Shweta Taneja is an award-winning author writes science and fiction for kids and adults. Her bestselling books include *They Made What? They Found What?* on amazing scientists of India; graphic novel *Krishna: Defender of Dharma*, and critically-acclaimed fantasy fiction series *Anantya Tantrist Mysteries* which is currently being made into a film. Her sci-fi short story *The Daughter That Bleeds*, was shortlisted in the prestigious French award Grand Prix de l'Imaginaire, and was awarded Editor's Choice Award (Singapore). She is a Charles Wallace Writing Fellow (United Kingdom) and has given talks at international conferences including WorldCon (Dublin), Eurocon (Amiens) and the Cartoon Museum (London). Her work has been translated to Kannada, French, Romanian, and Dutch.

She is a habitual tea-drinker, nature wanderer, and birdwatcher and has recently upgraded her laugh to evil. Connect with her online with her handle @shwetawrites or log onto www.shwetawrites.com.

# KUNGFU AUNTY VERSUS GARBAGE MONSTERS

SHWETA TANEJA

Illustrated by BABAKIKI

talking CUB

An Imprint of Speaking Tiger Books

TALKING CUB

125A, Ground Floor, Shahpur Jat,
Near Asiad Village, New Delhi 110049

First published in paperback in Talking Cub
by Speaking Tiger Books 2023



ISBN: 978-93-5447-528-3

eISBN: 978-93-5447-545-0

10 9 8 7 6 5 4 3 2 1


Typeset in Alegreyat by Jojy Philip
Printed at Sanat Printers, Kundli

*Dedicated to*

*Varun Taneja*
*Sibling supreme*

# CONTENTS

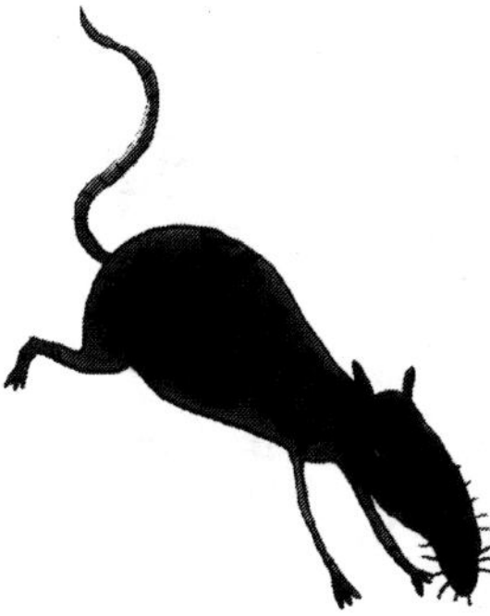

# HOW NOT TO SAVE YOUR DAD

Can you help me?

I'm Kabir, 9, and a goalkeeper in Pretty Public School's Junior Trashball team. A month ago, that was all I was. And I liked it that way, thank you very much. Now however, I'm in a tornado of torrid trouble.

It's Trash Rajah's birthday, you see. Every year, it's celebrated with virus-infested trashbombs and noxious firecrackers at the Supremely Vile Stadium. The stadium sits on top of the holy mountain of garbage, Puke Peak, in the middle of Lethal Lake.

I'm in position, defending my goal. The problem is what's behind me. It's my Dad. Yup, you heard that right. Can you see him? He's chained far back to a pole, his arms and legs dangling over the precipice. Under him are the poisonous waters of Lethal Lake. If you listen closely, you can hear him screaming.

I can't focus on that for facing me are a gaggle of squalid, smelly garbage monsters. They're snarling, sputtering spit, smelling their farts and armpits and squawking.

They're amused and they are sloshed on rotten cola. All the myriad variety of these nasties have one thing in common. They carry trashbombs in their jaws, hands, claws and giant nostrils.

They are all aiming the trashbombs at Dad.

One hit and he will fall into Lethal Lake and choke on its world-renowned toxic waters. Probably chewed to little bits by the plastocrocs that are swarming below him excitedly.

I shiver in my underpants. The only thing that stands between Dad and the monsters is me. And I'm not *that good* a goalkeeper.

The monsters move their collective limbs and jaws. A flurry of misshapen trashbombs hurtle towards us. I lunge to one side of the goal hoping to protect Dad, wondering where my sister Lila is.

As usual, my pesky little sister has done her favourite deed—a Vanishing Act. She's planning something. I just know it. I hope it's nothing to do with that troublemaker traitor Kungfu Aunty who has made our peaceful life a living hell.

You might have a younger sister or brother and you may think what's so bad about having one? Well, you haven't met Lila. She is the nosiest, most annoying creature on the planet. You might like to play trashball or swim in pig swill, but Lila, her hobby is to *rebel*. Yeah, you got that right. Her hobby is the reason Dad was kidnapped and is going to die a horrible, chewed-to-bits death.

It's. All. *Her*. Fault.

For she's the one who found Kungfu Aunty. But to know how *exactly* it's all her fault, I have to start from the beginning, for you don't know what happened, do you?

# THE TRASHBALL SMASHER

A month ago, on a normal Tuesday trashball practice day, my only worry was my oxyhelm.

It was a wonderfully muggy day. The playground at my school, Pretty Public School, had been freshly littered with soggy paper, broken glass, rubble and leftover food.

In keeping with the Directives of the Government, the trees that edged the playground were burnt a night before, so that a charred, nasty smog floated in the air, making it hard to see. Polythene bags and rags hung on the branches, artfully placed by Gardener Kaka.

In the flowerbeds, the burning leaves and debris simmered slowly, creating purplish smoke.

It was quite a sight. I wasn't happy though. My regular oxyhelm had been punctured and I was using my mother's oxyhelm, which was... well, you will find out in a second, anyway.

'Come on, Kab!' hollered Meera Kudur, the defender and my best friend. She flanked Tanay Bolt, our striker, who was playing against us today. He gave the trashball a kick. It vaulted towards the goal, at a hundred kilometres per hour.

'Block it, Kab!' snapped Meera, her ponytail swerving impatiently.

'No, no, no—' I craned my neck and barreled towards the trashball, urging Mom's oxyhelm to behave itself.

The sudden movement caused my oxyhelm to spout hundreds of needles. The trashball sank into these needles and lodged itself comfortably on the top of my head.

*Phissss*, it said sadly. The trashball dissolved around my helmet, dripping goo.

'Oh no,' I said.

Meera reached me, hands on knees. '*Again*?' Through my face shield, she looked green and gooey, thanks to the muck dripping on the visor of my oxyhelm.

'I will drown you in sparkling water!'

The threat came from Virat Namra, the well-built captain of the Junior Trashball team. He strode towards me, with a mean expression and meaner muscles that twitched threateningly. His burly best friends and notorious homework snatchers, Ishani and Ayaan, huddled closely behind.

Virat poked a big, muscled finger into my chest. 'This is the *second* trashball you've destroyed!' he said.

'Soap scrubber!' threatened Ayaan.

'Shampoo sparkler!' repeated Ishani.

'It's not my fault! It's my oxyhelm,' I countered.

'We all wear oxyhelms,' pointed out Vedika Dutta, our soft-spoken math genius, who was the team's forward. 'Only yours attacks and gobbles trashballs.'

'It's Mum's,' I sighed. 'I'm wearing it because mine ripped.' I wiped off gooey remnants of the trashball from my oxyhelm's visor. 'It *hates* trashballs.'

Meera's sharp nose crinkled in sympathy. Everyone knew about my mother. The rebellious, eccentric scientist, Dr Bhava Zarby. A green activist and cleanliness-obsessed human, she had made it her life's mission to invent machines that would help humans protect themselves from diseases and pollution. Most of her inventions had been outlawed after Pretty City had come under Trash Rajah's rule.

The oxyhelm had been one of her earlier inventions. It absolutely abhorred garbage and became a hedgehog whenever it came in touch with any kind of trash, producing needles and acid to dissolve it. I could even hear it fizzing a happy tune as remnants of soggy food dripped off its sodden needles.

'Is it even legal to use it?' asked Vedika, her eyes barely visible behind the glasses and the visor she wore.

'Guys, I hear some—' said Ishani.

'I don't care about legalese,' Virat snapped. 'You remove that psycho trash-eating 'helm of yours or you're out.'

'I can't play without an oxyhelm!' I cried.

'Then don't!'

'This is unfair, Virat,' countered Meera. Virat turned and growled at her. Though in my class, Virat was a year old, a head taller and beefier than everyone else. He wasn't used to being talked back to.

'What did *you* say?' the captain glowered, his nose inches away from Meera's face.

'Look, Virat,' sighed Vedika, 'It's the finals next month at Trash Rajah's birthday. The only way we can win against Daffodils is if we practice. *All* of us, together.'

'Fine, then ask *him* to remove his 'helm,' smirked Virat. 'Or is he too cowardly to do it?'

I stared at Virat. It wasn't illegal to remove your oxyhelm, but it was lethal. Pretty City's air was too toxic to breathe for humans. The oxyhelm was the only thing that protected us from Particulators and Virulates, Trash Rajah's elite airborne squad made of carbon particles and meta viruses. Without an oxyhelm, they would find an entryway to my lungs. I would be a coughing, asthmatic mess in an hour and would probably have to be hospitalized. Of course, Virat knew all this.

'I don't want to be sick,' I said.

'Then. Don't. Play.'

'Guys—'

'You will either play without the 'helm or you will leave. NOW!'

'Virat!' shouted Ishani.

'What?' he answered, glowering.

'*That*,' said Ishani. Her shaky finger pointed to something up in the sky. Everyone looked in the direction. Tiny black specks streamed through the smog. A distant hum thundered above.

'A whole swarm of fatflies?' said Vedika.

'Trash Rajah's army?' I shook. 'Why are they coming here?'

'Why should we care?' said Meera, who was always braver than me. 'We have given them Holy Offerings. They can take it and leave.'

'Umm, we—we haven't.'

The Pretty Public School's Junior Trashball team turned as one to stare at Dhruv Chowdhury, Lila's classmate, two years younger to us.

'You didn't *what*?' hollered Ishani who was Dhruv's elder sister. 'Mom made a ten-kilogram Carrion Chocolaty Cake last Tuesday!'

'Fatflies love rotten cake as a Holy Offering,' approved Tanay.

Every evening before play day, one of us got rotten dessert from home and placed it in a vestibule at the entrance of the playground. The Holy Offering was a bribe to the local Fatfly Army Station. If we did that, the fatflies would not come and play with us. If we didn't...oh well. I shuddered.

'So? Where is the rotten cake?' shouted Virat. A deafening buzz surrounded us. A dark shadow drew upon us as the swarm of giant fatflies came nearer.

'I...I was really hungry last evening and I...'

'You ate—' Ishani cried, '—the rotten cake meant for the fatflies army?'

'Yes,' mumbled Dhruv, looking at his shoes. 'I...I'll give them twice the cake tonight.'

'That won't help us! They will chomp us to bits before that!' shouted Virat. The army was on top of us now, an ominous black cloud covering half the playground.

'I think,' said Vedika, 'our best plan is to run.'

'*Run*!' agreed Meera.

Everyone moved together, sprinting across the ground, heading towards the exit gate at the far end. Dark shadows grew. The fatflies spread like ink in the murky sky. I ran, already out of breath, not daring to look up. Ahead of me, I could see Virat, who was already at the gate, followed by Meera and the few others.

A few fatflies dropped down in front of me and snapped their long black tongues. I screeched to a halt, heart hammering. Each was the size of a human head, their tennis-ball eyes bulging out, their antennas like thin swords. They wore a uniform made of metal scraps sewn together.

'Atten-*tion*,' said a shrill voice.

Ahead of me, all of my team had been forced to stop. More fatflies descended, circling around all of us, buzzing menacingly, pushing us backwards. We took steps back, till suddenly, we all huddled together somewhere in the centre of the playground, surrounded by the menacing Fatfly Army on all sides.

# THE WORST SISTER IN THE WORLD

It was the biggest fatfly horde I had ever seen. There were hundreds of them. Some hovered above ground glaring at us, some settled in the mushy ground, flicked their tongue on rotten stuff, while others circled around us. Their slat-coloured wings thundered, their armour gleamed, their antenna waved like swords. Their sizes varied—from the size of a mouse to a large dog, overfed on rotten goodies that humans provided them. They all buzzed together, mean, and big, and deafening.

'Atten-*tion*,' said a shrill voice. A tiny fatfly pulled up in front of us. His eyes were deep red in colour, his wings gilded with gold. He wore a chainmail made of gold and silver. He sat on a golden chariot pulled by two giant dragonflies. I would have laughed if I didn't feel dizzy with fear.

'We are named Captain Aurus Redfly,' he said. I had heard of Captain Redfly before. Head of the most feared battalion of the Fatfly Army, he had a nasty reputation. I stood still, hoping the fatflies would soon lose interest in me and I could escape back home.

'Who was the Food Provider for the Holy Offering?' asked Redfly. His voice boomed through the mike he used.

'I...I...sir,' said Dhruv. The kid shivered, his oxyhelm shuddering; his chubby face was shiny with sweat inside.

'Well?' asked Redfly. 'Where is Aurus's food?'

'I...'

'You know the punishment for not bringing us Holy Offering?' boomed Redfly. He pulled out a scroll, unraveling it with his rear leg. 'Dhruv Chowdhury, under section 377A of Pretty City Absolute Law, you are being arrested for willful Non-Delivery of Eatables to Trash Rajah's Fatfly Army.'

He flicked his thin hairy arm and hundreds of fatflies drew up, bee-lining towards Dhruv. I stepped back, and almost bumped into Ishani, who stood still behind me.

'Dhruv!' she mumbled.

'Don't leave me, Didi!' cried Dhruv, stumbling as fatflies started to close in on him.

'Please, he made a mistake,' cried Ishani, tears rolling off her round face. The fatflies were now focused on Dhruv. My teammates quietly started to leave. I saw my opening, and pushing Ishani, dashed towards the gate behind the others.

A part of me felt guilty for leaving Dhruv and Ishani, but what could I do? It was Dhruv's fault. He had broken the law, so he had to take the punishment. Everyone needed to follow laws or they will be punished. It was the way of the world.

Escaping the crowded circle, I exited the playground, already wondering what Dad had made for dinner. And then I remembered.

Lila, my younger sister.

I had left her at the swings. My heart sank into my shoes.

'Oh, nonono,' I said, turning around. In the middle of the playground, the fatfly whirlpool surrounded Dhruv. Ishani stood a few metres away from them, sobbing helplessly. The others, like me, had exited and made it home. I ran to the swings on the far side of the playground.

Oh! How I hated looking after my sister. Since Dad worked late on Tuesdays, I had to babysit her at the playground while I practiced.

I couldn't go back home without her. Dad would get furious.

The swings were empty. No Lila. As usual she had done a Vanishing Act—she could never really follow rules. She wasn't at the tire park or the jungle gym, either.

'Has anyone seen Lila?' I stopped a couple of Lila's classmates. They shook their heads.

'Lila!' I shouted. The fatflies buzzed, making it noisy. 'Where are you?'

The playground was now deserted except for the fatflies and Dhruv. Instead of descending on Dhruv, the fatflies had reorganized themselves into a vertical line—a long black wall reaching the skies.

A panicked thought struck me like a thunderbolt. I whipped around to look at the giant defence wall, bile rising up my throat.

Two small figures faced this wall. One was Dhruv and the other, in front of Dhruv, was my little sister. Shorter than Dhruv, she stood tall.

Her oxyhelm, green with white daisies painted on it, was too big for her small head.

'Leave him alone!' roared Lila. Her short black hair danced inside the oxyhelm as she brought out something that looked like a sword out of her skirt belt.

Oh yes, that's the other thing I had to tell you. My little sister loves playing the hero. I thundered towards her, my anger making me forget that I was heading straight into furious fatflies.

'Little human,' trilled Captain Redfly, whipping his two dragonflies. 'Don't you know it's Aurus's meal time?'

'Lila!' I shouted. 'Come on, we have to leave.'

'Please don't go! Don't leave me! I beg you!' sobbed Dhruv.

'Please leave our dessert! Aurus begs you, little human!' Redfly whistled like a pressure cooker. It was a laugh. The Captain flicked his foreleg, pleased with his joke. The fatflies rose up, humming together, ready to attack.

This so didn't look good.

# LILA'S SECRET WEAPON

Lila didn't need to do this. Even Ishani, Dhruv's sister, had been sensible and gone to the exit, waiting at a safe distance for it to get over. Trust Lila to try and play a hero.

'Grab the humans!' shrilled Redfly. The still wall of fatflies buzzed into activity, spiralling around Lila and Dhruv, till I couldn't see either of them.

'Oh, no! Oh, no!' I yelped, running towards them. I grabbed a rusted metal rod from a flower bed and plunged into the mayhem.

'Lila!' I said swatting at the mass of black fatflies. My oxyhelm spouted needles and zinged ecstatically. I whacked one fatfly that whizzed towards me, kicking another, my hands shaking.

'Take that, you hairy freak!' shouted Lila.

Smack! Pow! Pfft!

There were too many of them. I struggled, shooting, hitting, hurtling through the constant flux of fatflies. Their buzz grew louder and louder. The sky became dark and murky.

'Lila!'

A fatfly inserted its proboscis into my oxyhelm. Phissss, it cried sadly. Oho. Puncture. That meant my lungs were breathing toxic air. My eyes started to see black. I coughed, gripping the rod drunkenly. The fatflies swerved, missing my blows. I tried to hit one. I missed. There were too many. I sank onto my knees. I was surely going to die here, trying to save my Vanishing Act of a sister.

Phssss. Phssss. Phiss. Phisss. Srrrrrr. Srrrrrr. Phsss. Phsss. Srrr. Srrr.

I saw a faint light at the far end of the endless darkness that surrounded me. The light turned into a small human body. Lila emerged, squirting fairy dust from a sparkling wand. The shining dust hit the fatflies and they started to slow down, become sluggish, zigzagging midair, confused, banging into each other. Two seconds later, *plop*, they fell to the ground, becoming still. Zzzzzzz...

'*What*—?' I frowned, trying to shake off the hallucination.

Even though I hit my deflated oxyhelm with my fist and rattled it, Lila continued to spray fairy dust. Fatflies dropped off on the ground, snoring all around us. Dhruv lurked behind her, clapping his hands and grinning, oxyhelm badly dented.

I was definitely dreaming this.

'Bhaiya,' said Lila, hovering on top of me. Her wand leaked sparkle dust. Her cotton dress was blackened with muck. Her oxyhelm lay tilted on her shoulders. She grabbed my hand and tugged. 'I think we should leave.'

I didn't need another reminder. Even if this was a dream, it was good way to go. I got up, grabbed my sister and Dhruv's hand and ran towards the exit gate.

'Stop!' Captain Redfly descended from his chariot in front of us. The chariot wobbled, pulled by one dragonfly. The other snored on the ride's ceiling.

'Little human!' he snarled, 'Aurus shall shower you with rotten wrath!'

Lila pointed her wand towards Trash Rajah's Captain. Captain Redfly swerved the chariot quickly, and darted away into the smog, vanishing.

Lila walked, her hand holding mine and Dhruv's. We met Ishani outside the playground. She thanked us and put her arms around her chubby brother, sobbing. I kickstarted my polluting hoverboard. It spat carbon dioxide and carbon monoxide into the air behind.

'What was that *thing*?' I asked as soon as we were riding into the late afternoon traffic. She shook her head, saying nothing.

Our house was three roads away from school, but it took us half an hour, as traffic jammed the roads—another law by Trash Rajah. As human citiziens of Pretty City, it was our duty to ensure we kept pollution levels high. Rajah's airborne armies loved carbon dioxide, monoxide, benzene and especially formaldehyde. So, no human could walk or cycle, especially in the morning and evening. All adult humans used cars to drive up and down and across the city, while all kids had special pollution-creating hoverboards they used to commute from playgrounds and schools.

Parking my hoverboard on the porch of my home, I ran up, ringing the doorbell. Dad's lanky frame hung in a hologram, his face deflated into a frown.

We must have looked a sight.

'Dad,' said Lila, 'Bhaiya's oxyhelm got punctured!'

'What, *again*?' The hologram's frown became deeper.

'It's not *my* fault,' I protested. 'It's *her* fault!'

'How can it be Lila's fault, Kabir, if your oxyhelm is damaged? And what is *that* stuck to the helmet?' Dad's hologram pointed to my oxyhelm.

'We had a scuffle,' I said vaguely, sneaking past the disapproving copy of my father into the disinfectant chamber. Somehow, I suspected if I told him it was the remains of fatflies, he would ban me to eternity. I put Mom's moody oxyhelm next to my punctured one. We disinfected and entered the living room to meet our real Dad. He frowned uncannily like the hologram, his face pinched like a raisin.

'Kabir, you look like you've been bitten,' Dad said. He pushed his spectacles up the bridge of his nose and kneeled in front of me, pointing to my ankle. It was swollen. 'AntiRote for you.'

'Not me, *Lila*!' I protested. AntiRote was a yucky puke-tasting medicine which protected humans from monster bites. 'I went to save *her!*'

'You'll both get AntiRote, just to be safe.' Behind him, the television flashed noisily. Granny Gee, Mum's mother, who lived with us, stared at its ancient screen, her ear close to the television.

'Granny!' said Lila. She grabbed my hand and made her way to the living room. Dad followed, grumbling, before thankfully heading to the kitchen. 'Listening to the news again, are you?'

'What a dufus!' said Granny Gee who was a little deaf. She pointed to the television. The news anchor of Trash News was a nattily dressed monsterquito called Ma Skedo. The monsterquito excitedly buzzed about Trash

Rajah's upcoming birthday celebrations. On screen was also the human representative, Mayor Junkfan. He droned about how the whole city had to be involved to prove their love for their Rajah, especially humans.

'Be generous and leave extra rotten food to support the Fatfly Army. Drive longer hours to pollute and proudly serve wholesome toxic meals to our Particulator brethren.' Mayor's advice ended with positive stories. Of how Daffodil Private School was busy cooking a special feast for Trash Rajah—a massive virus-infested rotten pork. As usual, they wanted to win the trophy for the Best School in the City.

'Bring me a fly swatter!' hollered Granny Gee, hitting the television with a spatula. 'I want to flatten filthy traitors!'

I sighed and pulled her back. She sat on the sofa, muttering and eyeing the television suspiciously.

Granny Gee had dementia. Dad told us she grew up in a time before Trash Rajah became the king.

At that time, when Granny was young and Mom and Dad were my age, humans ruled Pretty City, but faced a massive problem.

Over years, humans had produced a lot of trash, which was thrown into Lethal Lake. This pile of garbage had become the mountain of Puke Peak. The lake and air had become so polluted that the humans were getting infectious diseases, couldn't breathe and were dying.

Trash Rajah, who was human once, promised the citizens that if they elect him, he will eat their garbage. The people agreed. If someone could tackle their garbage problem, that would be great. So, Trash Rajah became king of our city. He ate the trash humans produced. However even his appetite was not enough. He created a garbage-eating army to eat more and more of the trash. A few years later, his army had become big and bloated.

Now, the trash that people produced was not enough to feed this army. So Trash Rajah made laws: The garbage monster army was helping humans by eating their trash, so humans had to produce more trash to feed the garbage monsters.

It made complete sense to me. After all, if humans had asked for help from Trash Rajah, they should feed his army. It was our duty.

Poor Granny. She didn't know this. How Trash Rajah actually protected us. How garbage monsters were important. Without them, we would die.

Granny was always doing illegal things. Like asking me and Lila to have a bath, or, ugh, sprayed us with perfume. Cleaning your body had become illegal years ago.

Lila snuck up to Granny and gave her a big fat kiss on her wrinkled cheek. Ugh. I headed to the kitchen to help set the table.

“Why were you around garbage monsters?’ Dad asked waving a daal-filled ladle at me. I gulped, frozen, not sure what to say.

‘I went to save Dhruv, Dad,’ Lila entered the kitchen and faced Dad. ‘He didn’t make an offering so the Fatfly Army attacked him. That’s not right.’

‘Lila, you’re not supposed to interfere!’ Dad frowned at us. ‘Kabir, why didn’t you stop her?’

‘I—’

‘Dhruv is my friend, Dad!’ said Lila. ‘He’s in my class and Ruchira Ma’am told us to help friends.’

‘She attacked the fatflies—’ I began.

‘Long live citronella!’ hollered Granny from the living room.

‘—with a weapon.’

‘What?’

‘A *weapon*, Dad!’ I said triumphantly. Finally my parent was listening to my sensible reasoning. ‘It was a wand that sends out sparkles.’

A dish clattered to the floor. Dad stared at us as rotis stared back at him from the floor.

'You *attacked* them?' cried Dad. Lila eyed her flip-flops. 'Show me this weapon, please.'

Lila went to the living room and brought out the wand. I had been right. It was a thick pencil-like wand with a shower head. Papa took it from Lila and stared at it for a little too long.

'You went to Mom's lab,' he said softly.

That got me. Dad speaking softly means he is too angry to yell. The angrier he gets, the softer his voice becomes. If he's so mad that someone's going to get grounded for life, he goes silent. I beamed. This was a rare occasion. Dad rarely got angry with Lila. Usually, I was the one who faced the wrath of his silences.

Lila had done something we had been told definitely, certainly NOT to do. Our mother's laboratory, in the basement of our home, was forbidden with a big 'F'. FORBIDDEN. No one was allowed to go in there.

'I...I wanted to see what Mom made,' said Lila, shuffling her feet. She eyed the shattered plate that lay on the floor.

'You're in big trouble, young lady,' whispered Dad. 'You'll have your dinner and AntiRote—*both of you*—and go to sleep. You are grounded for two weeks.'

'That's unfair,' I protested. 'I have to prepare for my game on Trash Rajah's birthday! She used this weapon, not me!'

'It's not a weapon, it's a Kungfu,' countered Lila.

'You used a Kungfu?'

Oho. Dad's voice had become a faint whisper. Dad grabbed the wand, eyeing it with a look of horror. He glared at Lila. No words. *Mute*. Not a good sign *at all*. He picked up the rotis, turned back to focus on his daal. He slapped the ladle angrily, daal sloshing everywhere.

'What's a Kungfu?' I mouthed, looking at Lila. She shrugged. Poor girl looked like she was about to cry. She wasn't used to Dad being angry at her.

'It's not her fault, Dad,' I said. 'She found it by accident. She didn't know about this Kungfu. What is a *Kungfu*?'

Dad turned back and glowered at us both. 'I'm *not* entertaining any more questions from either of you,' he whispered. 'Tomorrow it's school and back home. No playground, no friends. *Straight. Back. Home.* Do you understand me?'

Dad angrily slapped rotis on our plates. We ate silently. Granny Gee broke the silence with a giggle or a swear word. I chewed vegetables thoughtfully, wondering what was it about this Kungfu that had made Dad so angry that he had forgotten to give us AntiRote for the monster bites.

# UNEXPECTED SCHOOL HOLIDAY

The next morning the school courtyard filled with students, blocking the entrance to the main building. Lila head-butted her way in, dragging me. Squiggling between people, we reached the front. The main entrance doors were firmly shut. A line of bloatrats flanked them.

Behind them, a sign dangled on the door handle.

'Humans, no go! Cleanorist at loose! Captain Aurus Redfly is investigating with Special Squad,' said one of the bloatrats. It was a

CLOSED TILL FURTHER NOTICE

By the Order of

AURUS REDFLY

*Newly-Appointed Captain*

*Anti-Cleanorist Special Squad*

*Pretty Public School District*

Cleaning violations and cleanorist activities suspected. Please comply with the investigations of Anti-Cleanorist Special Squad

dog-sized rat, with black beady eyes and a snout that hung like a hotdog.

'But...but this school is one of the filthiest in the city!" said Principal Ashraf. She stood ahead of us, wringing her hands nervously. 'Our Gardener Kaka's mess-making efforts were awarded by Trash Rajah last year.'

She stood with Gupta Sir, our mathematics teacher, who was built like a multiplication sign.

Lila pulled out something from her bag. It looked like a flute, but I knew better. One part of it looked too sharp.

'Is that another Kungfu?' I whispered. I pulled her arm back, trying to grab it. 'Give it to me!' She tussled with me.

'Trash Rajah's Education Ministry's Charter for Pretty Public School forbids any army activity on school premise,' said Gupta Sir. I didn't know what a charter was, but it definitely sounded like a good reason to open the door. I tried to get my hand on the flute Lila held. She kept dancing away.

'No!' snarled another bloatrat with larger, beadier eyes. 'Anti-Cleanorist Special Squad recognizes no governmental charter. When it comes to combating cleaning threats, we are the best!'

'And pray tell us what threat do you perceive from school kids?' This was from Ruchira Ma'am, Lila's class teacher.

'Yesterday, an Army Captain was attacked by a terrorist group wielding a mysterious weapon in the school's playground.'—Wait. Were they calling Lila a cleanorist? All she had done was protect her friend! Lila growled. I glared at her.—'The premises need to be searched thoroughly. This is of utmost importance in order to secure our city.'

'There must be some mistake,' cried Principal Ashraf. 'We protect our school grounds very well. There is no security threat here.'

'Protection is very important,' nodded the slightly smaller bloatrat. It sharpened its tooth with a knife, using it as floss. 'School closed. Go back, humans.'

'I will complain to the Education Ministry,' said Gupta Sir. He turned, addressing us. 'Children, please head to your homes today. Your parents will be informed when the school reopens.'

'But this is unfair!' cried Lila.

'Lila!' I tried to grab her. 'We need to leave!'

'This is *wrong*,' said Lila. With a sudden violent shake, Lila wiggled out my grip. She plunged on all four, as the teachers looked on, too surprised to stop her. She swung her hand that held the sharp flute. 'Lila, no!' I exclaimed.

The jab's pointy edge hit one of the bloatrats in the middle of his paw, lodging itself there. He looked at Lila, and a moment later, fell with a thud onto the floor. I waited for a scream, but none came. Instead, it snored.

Seeing their comrade fall, the other three bloatrats snarled. They jumped on Lila. Their sharp teeth gnashed.

'Ygh!' I shouted, running into the fight, followed by Meera and Ishani. We tumbled together onto the ground, kicking, biting, clawing, chewing and chomping.

*Crunch. Pow. Poof. Pfft.*

'Stop it!' cried Principal Ashraf, 'They have guns!'

My oxyhelm, the one which belonged to my mother, spouted needles. It trilled with happiness, injecting three bloatrats with something that slowed them, like Lila's jab had done. But the bloatrats were bigger, scarier and meaner than fatflies.

Five minutes later, the fight was over. A bloatrat plastered me to the ground, pushing the muzzle of a pistol into my face—with virus-infected slugs as bullets. Another pushed Lila's face into the mud. I heard Meera grunt and Ishani gasp. Our oxyhelms were broken, bites and scratches and wounds covered our bodies. Principal Ashraf looked at me with an expression of disbelief. And fear.

A few minutes later, the Anti-Cleanorist Special Squad started their investigation and we walked out on the road.

A medical attendant leaned over me on the sidewalk and shook her head.

'One week of AntiRotes.'

'Did you see, Bhaiya?' cried Lila, grinning as another attendant patched up a scratch on her shoulder. 'I found this Stun Jab in the Kungfu collection! It worked!'

I groaned. As I said, my little impulsive monkey of a sister is the bane of my life. And this was just the beginning. I found the true extent of her deceptive plan a few days later.

# HOW TO FIGHT A PSYCHO ROBOT

It was Wednesday, a week later. Our school had remained closed thanks to Lila's antics. Principal Ashraf had complained and applied for reopening the school to the Education Ministry. The ministry was however busy with upcoming celebrations of Trash Rajah's birthday and yet to reply.

I was in a sour mood. I lay curled up in the living room, reading Wild Wuss, my favourite anti-hero series. Wild Wuss was my kind of a hero. Whenever bad things happened near him, he snuck away. 'Want to live longer?' he would say, 'stay out of trouble.'

Unlike my pesky sister. She was the reason the playground was shut, my trashball practice suspended. Why did she have to go and save Dhruv? Rules were rules and we had to follow them. She should have let the Fatfly Army deal with Dhruv. That was the right way. The Wild Wuss way. No need to be too nosy or brave. Be still, hide. Be nimble footed. That's the reason I made a good goalkeeper. Keep out of trouble, observe and stay safe.

My tummy felt uneasy. Nope, I wasn't hungry. This was a peculiar gnawing feeling that my sister was brewing trouble somewhere.

She had done the Vanishing Act again. Since morning, I had not seen her in the living room. Yup, definitely up to something.

Dad was busy thanks to Rajah's birthday. He worked at one of the Factory Farms on the other side of Lethal Lake. The Factory Farm had to work around the clock to produce batteries, cement, chemical, dyes, and petroleum to create pollutants to dump into Lethal Lake. A month before Trash Rajah's birthday, the Factory Farm worked all hours, keeping most parents busy. After all, Trash Rajah liked Lethal Lake to be fuming with extra noxious steam on his birthday.

I got up, unable to concentrate anymore thanks to my stomach and sister. Climbing up the stairs, I tiptoed to her room. It creaked open. The bed and the desk were empty. I frowned, turned and banged into something metallic.

'Eek!'

'Hi, Bhaiya!' said Lila, who wore a metallic armour that covered her from head to toe. Her voice echoed.

'What are you upto?'

'I found the actual Kungfu!'

'What?' I whispered back, wondering why I was whispering. 'How?'

'Mom told me.'

'Mom?'

Had Lila gone bonkers like Mom? Mom had passed away soon after Lila was born. I barely remembered her. Just her callused hands and a wild look in her eyes. Much like Lila, now that I thought about it.

'Do you want to come?' she asked, twirling her hair.

Classic Lila. She never answered the question you asked her.

'Where?'

'To Mom's lab,' she said. She patted around her armour, and produced a bunch of keys. I sputtered. Those were the keys that Dad kept in his bedside table drawer.

'We are not allowed to go to Mom's lab, Lila!' I explained, trying to offer the wisdom of logic to my hare-brained sister.

She shrugged and walked past me to go downstairs. I stood undecided, looking at her in the corridor. After a moment's hesitation, I followed. After all, I was the elder brother and had to make sure Lila would not get into trouble. I also wanted to find out what she meant when she said Mom told her about Kungfu.

We went down to the basement, facing the locked laboratory door. Lila switched a torchlight which danced in the vestibule. With the practiced ease of a professional thief, Lila chose the right key from the bunch she held, put it into the locked door and turned it.

The door creaked open.

It was dark and menacing. Lila hopped down few more stairs after the door, heading into sheer darkness. I gulped, taking a step tentatively. It wasn't like I was scared. I just wanted to make sure I didn't head into something bad. There must have been a reason Dad stopped us from going here.

'You see?' asked Lila.

'What?' I cried. My toe hit something metallic. 'Owowowwowo!'

'This, Bhaiya!'

Lila pointed her flashlight at an ancient-looking refrigerator. The beam shook in excitement.

'You want me to see a freezer? Why?'

'Wait.'

She walked away. A second later, blinding light flooded the lab. I staggered. Something was very, very wrong.

The lab was the size of our living room and kitchen combined. A long hall with a two-feet wide long table at the centre. The walls on all sides were mostly covered with assorted cupboards and racks, all very neatly organized.

That wasn't the creepy part. The part that was very, very creepy was the fact that it was all spotlessly clean. The floor squeaked as I walked on it. Metal tables gleamed, their surfaces reflecting light. The glass jars in the shelves sparkled. Door knobs shone. Beakers and pipes and containers all looked spic and span.

Who was doing something as illegal as cleaning here? And why?

'Lila, this looks wrong,' I said. 'Lila?' I whipped around. And my sister was gone. I tiptoed like a chubby bloatrat, careful not to touch anything.

Something tickled my ear.

'Stop it, Lila!' I cried, swatting her fingers with my hand, heart hammering. 'We—aiyaaaaaa!'

My voice froze like it had touched a Yeti's bum. It hadn't been Lila who had tickled me. It had been a thing. The refrigerator that Lila had shown me had moved silently. And now it was behind me. It also had a long thin metal arm spouting from it. With a brush attached to it. I blinked my eyes rapidly.

A quiet whirr made the brush and the arm retreat into the freezer-creature. I croaked. The freezer moved again, silently circling me.

'Lila!' I whimpered. There was no answer. Tiptoeing around the fridge-thing, which I was sure was eyeing me, I noticed a small panel stuck to its body, an inch above the floor. I squinted to read.

**KUNGFU CLEANBOT™ VERSION 27**

Kungfu was a robot that cleaned? Invented by Mom? That didn't make sense. That would make Mom a cleanorist! No wonder Dad wanted to keep her lab a secret.

Everyone knew cleaning is sedition in Pretty City, punishable by immersion into Lethal Lake where oiliguanas and plastocrocs await tender human flesh. We hear this every day at school assembly.

The metallic monster whirred. I carefully inched away from it. In the bright lights, it had a smooth, matte finish. No visible buttons or handles. How did it work? It whirred again, flashing an orange beam of light on my body. I staggered backwards. A pair of O's emerged on the cleanbot's gleaming surface. They blinked. Eyes.

**COMPREHENSIVE CALCULATION CONCLUDED.**

The thing's voice boomed making me jump. Another O emerged below the 'eyes'. A mouth which shaped words.

**RADICAL CONTAMINATION DETECTED IN HOMO SAPIENS SAMPLE.**

'Choo! Begone you cleaning creep!'

**PROCEDURE TO COMBAT CONTAMINATION. STEP ONE, ION-SCRUBBING. STEP TWO, DEEP CLEANSING. STEP THREE, ODOUR RINSING. PROCEDURE TO COMMENCE IN FIFTEEN SECONDS.**

'Umm, hello,' I said, trying a different tactic. I had never spoken to a robot before, so didn't know what to say to it. A timer started on its boxy tummy. Orange numbers flickered.

**00.14**
**00.13**

**00.12**

**RADICAL CONTAMINATION ALERT!**

Now I wasn't sure what the word 'contamination' exactly meant, but something about the timer and the word 'alert' didn't sound right. I rapidly started to step back.

'Lila—' I called out. My pesky sister had done her Vanishing Act again.

**00.05**

**00.04**

**00.03**

'—we need to leave—*aaaaah*!'

The robot spun and spouted long thin arms, like snakes. They all ended with brushes of different kinds.

'Aiya!' I fell on the floor. The robot moved like a hurricane, two of its evil arms grabbing me by my shoulders. 'Leave me!' I cried. It didn't listen.

Metallic clasps gripped my arms and pulled me into the air. Yes, you read that right, straight into the air. My legs dangled.

'Aaaa! Leave me, you mopping lunatic!' I cried. The evil creature's eyes gleamed golden. Another pair of fork-shaped arms appeared and there was a loud pop. A thick pink bubble blew out from its fat belly.

*Plooooop!*

The bubble expanded around me. The room on the other side looked distorted and turned rainbow coloured.

**ION-SCRUBBING COMMENCING.**

*Suck. Suck. Sptt. Sptt.*

My body was pulled into this bubble. I started to scream, but I had a feeling that my voice was just echoing in the bubble room the evil monster had created. Five long toothbrushes, gleaming pink, full of bristles whirled towards me. The toothbrushes touched my body everywhere, scrubbing, brushing, stroking, rubbing.

I thought it would hurt badly. Instead, it tickled. I laughed madly as the brushes tangoed. They scoured. My chin, my arms, my legs, my neck. The brushes twirled tickling my underarms and knees.

As if this wasn't bad, a thick liquid started to fill up in the bubble.

'No, no!' Terrified, I felt choked, gulping the little air left inside the bubble. 'Cleaning is *illegal*!'

The robot released tiny metallic beetles that started to chomp on my clothes. This was the end.

Through the haze of the now purplish bubble, I saw the misshapen form of my sister. I tried to wave at her from between the tangle of arms of the cleanbot who held me quite firmly.

'Call Dad,' I gurgled.

'Kungfu Aunty!' said Lila. Her voice was muffled but clear. A beetle snuck into my ear. 'Do you want to see *Dragon Tail versus Snake's Paw* again?'

This was so classic Lila. I had given her a clear instruction. Call Dad and save me from the psycho-cleaning robot. Instead, she was *talking* to it. Calling it *Aunty*. And what was that about dragons and snakes?

I wriggled as a tentacle showered me with something nastily sweet. Ugh.

'Run, Lila! Save yourself!' I gurgled. If I was to go, at least I should try and save my silly sister. Maybe Dad and her would appreciate my end-of-life heroism.

Lila didn't respond. She pulled out a black book and waved it at the robot.

'It's your favourite one,' she said.

The robot's eyes deepened to the colour of black. A metallic arm bolted from its body and wrapped around Lila's little body, pulling her up.

'Let's go?' smiled Lila. Why was she so calm? I screamed from inside the bubble, mad at my sister.

**MOOOBIEEE. VEECEEARE.**

A compartment in the robot's box opened and gobbled Lila. She vanished!

'No...ugh!' I screamed silently, liquid filling my throat. How did you fight a psycho robot to save your sister?

# THE FASCINATING EFFECTS OF MARTIAL ARTS

It didn't look good. I was trapped in a bubble. Lila had gotten herself eaten by a sterilizing sadist. This was it. All my dreams of becoming the star goalkeeper, of winning the finals in the upcoming tournament were bust. The cleanbot glided deeper into the laboratory. I floated in the pink bubble like a frog in a balloon. My stomach churned. I wished I had listened to Dad's warnings and never entered this accursed lab. Like my hero Wild Wuss. He would have been smart enough to realize the basement was bolted for a lunatic lurked in it somewhere. I wished—

The cleanbot stopped and gurgled. Something plopped out of its stomach. I frowned. It looked like Lila. She got up and gave the robot a smile.

'Let's go!' she grinned.

What was happening? Do you think this is normal? For a little girl to be gobbled by a scrubbing machine and come out laughing? A robot arm extended and handed her a small black book. The same one she had shown it. I frantically waved my arms, trying to grab my sister's attention.

Lila took the book, ignoring me, and put it in a flat drawer-shaped machine in front of her.

A screen lit up. My brows creased. It looked like a garbled oval with a video playing on it. Two people wearing costumes and long ponytails were fighting. A movie. A martial arts movie.

POP!

The world around me crashed. I splatted on the floor. Scrambling up, I checked my body. Nothing was broken. Thanking my guardian angels, I checked once more and gasped.

I was *clean*! I mean not the way you would take a bath once a month, but *glistening* clean. I sniffed my underarms, horrified. They smelled like they had been sprayed with fresh, ugh, *flowers*.

'Did you like the lavender nano-scrub, Bhaiya? I asked Kungfu Aunty to do the one with bubbles. It tickles, no?'

Lila eyed me, as she sat curled up against the creepy robot's body like a cat. The robot's eyes were white slits now, a huge U-shaped smile on one panel of its cuboid body. It stared at the grainy picture rapturously, ignoring us. What had the psycho robot done to my sister?

'Lila,' I whispered, 'We need to go.'

'This is the best part, Bhaiya. Wait for it.'

She turned back to the television, pointing at something.

'What is?'

'The dragon is going to attack the village. The only person who stands against it is this girl, who learnt martial arts from her mom!'

'*What*?' I said. There you go. Don't you see? It's simply *impossible* to reason with my little sister. For most of the time, she lives in a galaxy which is gazillions of light years away from our reasonable one. I wondered again if a doctor had dropped her on her head when she was born. 'We need to *leave* now!'

'Oh fine. But you have to see something first.'

'There's another cleanbot here?' I squeaked, looking around, my belly dropping to the ground. She shook her head, got up, and headed to the far corner of the room, which was piled with dozens of books. All dust-free and well-organized. She took out a notebook.

‘This is Mom’s diary!’ she said excitedly, opening up the journal. There were pages after pages of scribbles and drawings. She stopped at one. It was a futuristic landscape. A blue-coloured lake with white clouds. Humans taking a walk around the lake, some swimming in the water. None of them were wearing oxyhelms or oxysuits.

“What’s this painting got to do with us?”

‘This is not imagination. This is how Mom imagined Pretty City could be, Bhaiya! Blue skies. No one wearing oxyhelms. Dustbins, biobins everywhere to compost waste. Recycling plants to deal with plastic. She imagined a new world where we did not need a garbage army to deal with our trash. We could do it ourselves. I’ve been reading Mom’s diaries and she invented so many things to make this dream work! That’s the reason she invented Kungfu. Don’t you see? Kungfu Aunty can save us from Trash Rajah and their armies.’

‘What are dustbins?’ I asked, which frankly was one of the million questions I wanted to ask as I stared at the pages.

‘Mom wrote they’re buckets you put your garbage in. Like rotten food, plastic, paper, anything that you don’t want to use.’

‘Why would you horde garbage like that?’ I muttered. That was again, so illegal. In Pretty City, you had to produce garbage to feed Trash Rajah’s army. That was the law we lived by.

‘So people remain clean and disease-free. But there’s more! See these drawings.’ She shuffled through new pages. ‘This is a special dustbin model. Biobins. A basic robot with sensors. Kungfu Aunty can also make us some! They seek, sort and destroy trash. Imagine, if we had a whole army of biobins, we could face—’

‘Are you *mad*, Lila? That’s rebellion! You’re thinking like a cleanorist!’

'But Bhaiya, imagine! We won't need oxyhelms or oxysuits. We don't need to feed the army with rotten food. We can be *free*!'

'Trash Rajah rules the city and protects us. In exchange, we feed his army with human-produced garbage. You have learnt this in your class. That's how it should be. You have to stay out of trouble, Lila!'

'No! Mom says we don't need to slave for Trash Rajah and his garbage monsters. We can deal with our own trash. We can be free!!'

'That's the reason she *died*.'

Lila and I twisted our necks, to look behind. Dad stood at the bottom of the stairs. His eyes were bloodshot. He didn't look angry. He looked scared. Like he had been crying.

'*What*?' I exclaimed. Before now, Dad had never told us about Mom. He came forward and sank to his knees, face to face with Lila and me. He tried to pull me into a hug. I squiggled away. 'How did Mom die?' I asked quietly.

Dad sighed and stretched out his arm to touch Kungfu's panel. The robot switched down, inert.

'Your mother was a genius,' he said, his voice full of grief. 'Before Lila was born, she and a group of others planned a revolt against Trash Rajah and his garbage monsters. The plan was to release biobins in the city to reduce his army's strength. However, before they could do it, they were betrayed by one of their team. Trash Rajah found out. Your mother—' his voice choked '—had just given birth to Lila. All of them were arrested and we never saw them again. I was told, she is...*not there* anymore.'

'Dad, we can fight the garbage monsters again! I have a plan!' exclaimed Lila. Dad shook his head.

'This model,' said Dad, pointing to Kungfu Aunty, 'is the last remaining cleanbot your Mom made. It's all gone.'

'No listen, Dad, I found out that there is a way—'

'No, Lila, *you* listen to me!' He pulled her and me into his arms, looking at both of us alternatively. 'I lost your mother to this madness. I cannot lose you both. Please, promise me you will not come back to the laboratory again.' He started to cry. I didn't know what to do.

'We promise,' Lila and I mumbled in unison, looking at each other.

I was glad that Lila had promised to leave the madness behind. I was yet to realize I had been wrong.

# A MYSTERIOUS MISCREANT

On Friday, Dad received an email from Principal Ashraf. Our school was finally going to reopen on Monday. Great. I couldn't wait. The week following the Kungfu episode had been exhausting. For a while, I had wondered what it would be like to have a city where I didn't need to wear an oxyhelm. Is that the city Granny Gee had grown up in? But Dad was right. Trash Rajah and his army were too strong. We would never stand a chance against them. Stay out of trouble. Yes, that was the sensible way to go. I was glad that Lila had listened to Dad.

Monday morning, I entered the school building, bounce in my step, ready to pursue my dream of winning the trashball junior league in Pretty City.

Immediately I knew something was horribly wrong. The building floor was sparklingly, spotlessly polished with no dust, no crumpled paper or plastic wrapper in sight. The graffiti on the walls had been rubbed off. There was no layer of dust on the cabinets, doors or the desks in our classrooms. The school was *spic and span.* It even smelled rather nice. *Lavender.* My heart sank.

Principal Ashraf rushed through the corridor, talking on the phone.. '...don't know how it happened!' she screamed. 'The whole school. Yes, the whole school has been argh... *sanitized*! You have...yes...the health minister is due to visit tomorrow. I don't care how difficult it is! I need three truckloads of garbage and rotten food here *instantly*...'

Gardener Kaka and other teachers rushed back and forth in the corridors. All of them had trash bags with them. They were hurriedly taking out rotten food, pieces of rubble, paper, plastic and throwing them around.

My heart sank into the floor. The Special Squad had been right. There was a cleanorist in the school.

Gupta Sir ushered all children into the assembly hall. I joined the wave, heading towards the assembly hall that was at the back of the building.

'Students of Pretty Public School, stand to attendance!' Principal Ashraf was already on stage. Her tied hair framed her head like little cobwebs. Virat and his floozies stood at the far end. I scuttled behind Meera who stood in line, in the middle.

'What did I miss?' I whispered. Even as I said it, a horrific idea had started to form in a dark, suspicious corner of my mind. Somehow,

I knew, I just knew, it was all related to my pesky sister. I didn't hear Meera's response as Principal Ashraf's voice boomed.

'Students, this is an emergency,' she said. 'As you may have noticed, over the weekend some hooligans have defiled our lovely school. We need to undo the criminal sanitization. It's wasteful and sinful to do away with trash! I cannot stress enough. Trash is precious to Pretty City's soldiers. Strictest action will be taken against whoever is responsible. If anyone knows anything, come to my office and inform us. To keep us all safe, the ministry has decided to close the playground, though they allowed the school to continue. Captain Redfly and his Special Squad will be patrolling the school grounds and playground today. I warn everyone not to go there as it's dangerous. All trashball and trashbomb practice is hereby suspended.'

As soon as Principal Ashraf walked off the stage, Meera turned and hugged me. I staggered, surprised.

'You are my hero, Kab!' she said emotionally. 'I don't know how you're doing it, but way to go!' She gulped. 'I will be at the playground to support you. We will show them!'

'Show them what?' I asked, stupefied. Why was Meera going to the playground when Principal Ashraf had just mentioned how dangerous it would be to go there? And why had she hugged me all dopey with hope? I whipped around and glared at my sister. She stood in the Junior line, a few rows down from me. She beamed and waved, whispering something to Dhruv and giggling as she left with her class. My annoying sister was up to something.

I began to walk towards her, when a long shadow fell on me. I looked up. Three senior boys from the trashbomb team surrounded me. Trashbomb was a rougher game than trashball. It involved throwing multiple heavy balls of trash across the field towards the goal. The messier the splash, the more chances of your winning. You needed wide shoulders and powerful biceps for all that heavy garbage lifting.

'That's brave,' said Vivaan Munshi, the captain of the trashbomb team. He had a heavy, adult voice. I gulped. 'I respect that.'

'You're the Junior team goalkeeper. Kabir, right?' asked Sajan Khan, patting me on the shoulder. A faint mustache cropped his upper lip, under his aquiline nose. 'You're being brave. We'll be at the playground after school to support you.'

Me? Brave? I smiled tentatively, taking a polite leave. I needed to find out—I banged into something hard. Virat glared at me, flanked by Ishani and Ayaan. He grabbed my shoulders, leaning till our heads touched.

'How are you doing it?' he growled.

'Doing *what*?' I frowned. Usually, I wouldn't have been this flippant to Virat, but the trashbomb team had just now assured me that they supported me. I glowered. He looked towards the seniors and back at me.

'Listen, you little toddle,' he whispered, digging his finger into my chest. 'You think I will let you take all credit for making sure we play? I know you're a coward. I. Want. To. Know. What. You. Know.'

'I'm making sure we play?' I gulped. From the corner of my eye, I signalled Meera to come to my rescue. Virat curled his fingers and turned it into a rather large fist, showing it to me.

'If you try and keep me out of this, I will crush you into a tin!'

My eyes transformed into saucers.

'But...I don't know—'

An hour later, I had a free period. I scurried through the corridor, wore my oxyhelm and oxysuit, exiting the building to rush to a shed outside the school. Lila had Ethics for Trash, a compulsory course sponsored by the Ministry of Civics and Politics. The class was taken by Miss Gnat Buzzbug, a special instructor from Trash Rajah's court, who talked about the duties of humans in Pretty City. Miss Buzzbug was a cat-sized monsterquito with a sword-length stinger and rounded eyes. She hated being in a classroom, so Principal Ashraf had created a smelly sump in a shed near the playground for her class.

I rushed to the door. Even the ramshackle shed looked clean today. Pond sewage, created lovingly by Gardener Kaka and much loved by monsterquitoes had been dried and levelled. It smelt of, umm, *flowers*. Lavender. Crinkling my nose, I found my sister at the far corner and waved at her, trying to catch her eye.

'As the authorities try to find the cleanorist,' Miss Buzzbug fizzed grimly, 'you all should focus on Trash Rajah's birthday bash. The

Ministry of Consumption has planned a special decay cake competition. What is their favourite flavour, little humans?

'Sewage Sludges!' shouted the class in unison.

'And Affluent Effluent!' hissed the teacher. 'Give them that and they will forgive all your transgressions. The nastier it is, the better they love it. Remember humans, your duty as a Pretty City citizen is to consume, waste and contribute to Rajah's vast armies. You—'

'Miss,' I interrupted. Miss Buzzbug squinted towards me. 'I need to urgently speak to my sister, miss.'

Miss Buzzbug cricked her proboscis. She played with the blood-red holy rag around her thin neck. 'During break.'

'But, miss, it's very, very, importantly urgent. *Please*.' Miss Buzzbug squinted and buzzed to the door, pulling my ear with her thin foreleg.

'Puny human, do you want me to bite you? For I haven't had my dose of blood yet.' I gulped and scuttled away.

Yes, there were mysteries to be solved, but not when a teacher wanted to give you malaria. I headed back to my own class and waited.

# LILA'S LITTLE SECRET

Time crawled by through Science, English and History. By Mathematics, I was sure everything was connected to Lila. My seniors being friendly. Meera's unusual hug. Virat's glare. Everything. Everything was connected to my annoying sister.

As soon as the school bell rang for afternoon break, I rushed out, beelining towards Lila's class. She huddled with Dhruv on a bench in the corridor, showing him a remote. I grabbed my little sister by her t-shirt, pulled her up, taking her aside.

‘Lila, why does Meera think I’m working on a plan that will allow us to practice trashball?’

Lila gave me a sly smile.

‘What’s going to happen at the playground?’ I asked furiously.

‘Kungfu Aunty will—’

‘That maniac metallic mess?’ My throat was suddenly dry. ‘What’s it got to do with *anything*? You promised Dad you will stay away from that monster. Listen, we can get into serious trouble...’ My throat felt dry. I took out a bottle of water and took a long gulp.

My sister continued to speak as if I hadn’t shown my disapproval. ‘—I promised Dad I wouldn’t go to the laboratory, but Kungfu Aunty came and met me. Two nights ago, as we watched a rerun of *Dragon Tail versus Snake’s Paw* again, she wanted to see my school.’

I sputtered, splashing water all over my uniform.

‘That psychopath is in our school?’

'Don't be mean to Kungfu Aunty, Bhaiya,' Lila frowned. 'She's nice.'

'Stop calling that maniac mess your aunty!'

Her face drooped.

'She was Mom's invention, Bhaiya,' Lila muttered, looking sad. 'She was proud of her as we should be.'

'Lila,' I sighed, 'Mom made something bad, okay? Cleaning is *illegal.* You know that?' I said. Suddenly, it hit me like an oncoming truck. I know I should have thought of it before. You would have, right? But somehow, I had just been so focused on my trashball strategy. 'Don't tell me it was *that robot* who cleaned up the school? Kungfu is the cle—' I lowered my voice, '—*cleanorist*?'

'I didn't ask her to, Bhaiya,' Lila shrugged. 'But I do like how our class smells today. It feels nice and fragrant.'

Confession here to you, dear readers. Though I would never tell my sister, even I liked how the school felt. I rather liked the sweet-smelling lavender. However, now wasn't the time to figure out why I was having these revolting feelings. I had to stop being looked upon as a hero who worked with a cleanorist.

'Why does Meera think I'm going to get the team to practice at the playground today evening?'

'Because of Dhruv,' she said, smugly.

'Dhruv?' I said.

'When Principal Ashraf said there will be no practice, Dhruv came to me to ask if Kungfu Aunty could help us. I asked her and—'

'What? Dhruv knows about the cunning cleanorist?'

'Of course,' shrugged Lila, 'He's my best friend. I also wanted to play at the jungle gym so I told him you and I will get Kungfu Aunty and she will protect us so we can all play.'

'*What? No way.* We can't unleash that maniac robot in the playground! After school, we have to take her back to the lab and lock her before Dad finds out.'

'You're right, Bhaiya,' she said. I blinked. Did Lila just agree with me? 'I thought you will not like it so I already told everyone that we won't go to the playground.'

'*What*?' I exclaimed.

'There you are!'

I whipped around. Sajan and Vivaan sauntered towards me. Sajan smiled as he swaggered towards us.

'You little piece of surface wipe,' he said, still smiling. He pulled me up towards the ceiling. My feet dangled. 'I hear there will be no practice anymore!'

'I ... !' I gulped.

'If we don't get to play in the playground, we will bomb *you* instead. You hear me?' growled Vivaan. Behind them, Virat, who had just seen this exchange, smirked. The two burly boys dropped me.

'Bhaiya,' said Lila after they had gone. 'I will take Kungfu Aunty home.'

'No, no, no!' I cried. 'She has to make sure we play in the ground!'

'But just now you said,' said Lila. She gave me an innocent smile, that felt like a trap. Like this was her plan all along.

'No, no, you were right, Lila,' I said, digging myself deeper into her trap, 'We have to practice, even if Captain Redfly doesn't approve. We need Kungfu Aunty to protect us while we play.'

'You're my hero,' Lila said, hugging me.

All right, I confess. It was self-preservation that made me do it. I'm no hero. I don't like to break rules or do illegal things. But if the alternative is someone breaking my bones, well, I had to choose the lesser evil, didn't I?

I was so naïve. Even in my most petrifying nightmare, I could not have imagined what happened at the playground. It was *way* worse.

# KUNGFU AUNTY KEEPS HER PEACE

Half an hour later, I dragged Meera, Dhruv and Vedika to the supplies room. It smelled of lavender.

Lila called out the evil reincarnation of a vacuum cleaner. Kungfu silently whirred into the room, looking bright and chuffed.

'Bhaiya, before we go to the playground, Kungfu Aunty wants to give us all something.'

'No!' I said, stepping back. Horror images of Kungfu's last gift, the lavender nano-scrub flashed in my mind. My friends looked at me in confusion. 'I mean, no, thank you. It's impolite to receive gifts from a cleanbot.'

'These are essentials, Bhaiya,' said Lila, a glint in her eye. On her signal, Kungfu's stomach became a ramp and a tumble of things rolled out. She picked up stuff and handed it to us all. Mine looked like a pencil. I frowned.

'Don't tell me. Are these all Kungfus?' I cried, 'You can't hand out weapons to—'

'Is someone still here?' We froze, standing still. Someone stopped outside the supplies room door, turned the handle. The door opened with a creak. In a jiffy Kungfu moved and stood in front of us, hiding us. Whoever peeked inside, mistook the cleanbot for a washing machine. They left.

'Let's go,' I whispered as soon as the footsteps faded away.

We put a blanket on top of the cleanbot and sneaked out the door, exiting through the rear of the school building.

Pretty Public School had been built much before someone had decided to extend it with a playground. The playground was not next to the building, but a hundred metres away, connected through a winding pathway that went behind the school. Today I was glad that was the case as we could sneak out of the school building unnoticed.

The gates to the playground were firmly shut. Four bloatrats sauntered from one side to another, lazily chewing rotgum. A long line of players stood at the entrance, waiting. From the far end, Sajan and Vivaan eyed me menacingly. This was such a bad idea.

We all wore our oxysuits—complete armours. I had insisted we do.

'It's hard to practice in oxysuits,' said Vedika. 'Why did you insist we do it?'

'He's pretending to be a hero,' smirked Virat. He reached out and pulled the blanket. 'A washing machine?'

'You're going to *wash* the fatflies army away?'

Kids tittered. Ignoring Virat, I wheeled the cleanbot in front of the gate. It was now or never. The muscled trashbomb team moved aside ominously, allowing me to go ahead. I squared my shoulders and swaggered up.

'Open up,' I said to the bloatrat at the gate. 'We want to practice.'

One of the bloatrats put his little claw up his nostril and moved his fingernail deep inside, bringing goo back to his big mouth. He sucked on the fingernail with a 'pccch' sound.

'This playground is closed,' he said.

'We have an offering for Captain Redfly,' I smiled, pointing to the cleanbot. The bloatrat's eye roved on its smooth platinum body. His fingernail was back digging in his fat nostril.

'Captain Redfly does like offerings, he does. What it is?'

'I will show it to the Captain,' I said. The bloatrat snarled. I stepped back.

'You tell the Captain that you were the reason he didn't get a treat for his army,' said Meera.

The bloatrats are beasts. They have sharp claws and spiky teeth that dig into flesh. However, they're not very well known for their brains. The bloatrat made a sucking sound. His lips scrambled like noodles. Thinking. Slowly. Very slowly.

'Go, give offering,' he finally said.

'Umm, Bhaiya...'

'Not now, Lila,' I said, holding her hand. 'We will take the offering into the playground. Come on, everyone.'

'Ah, no, no, no,' said Virat. 'The Junior Trashball team will wait here till you finish.'

I glared at him. He smiled. He knew I was hoping that all of us could go together and beg the army to let us play.

'I'll come with you,' said Meera. Vedika and Dhruv followed.

The gate creaked open. Six of us—me, Lila, Meera, Vedika and Dhruv and Kungfu—walked into the playground, oxysuits on.

The playground was a cesspool of smells. Bloatrats lay on top of mounds of garbage, squatting on top of each other. Monsterquitoes swam in dense, oily sumps. Fatflies buzzed lazily, scattered on top of a rotten food spread.

A feast was in full swing. Captain Redfly sat surrounded by fatflies, sitting on a mound of a giant feces-filled fruit cake. I gulped. This was such a big mistake.

We stopped with Kungfu a few feet away from the feast.

'Listen, Bhaiya...'

'Shh! Not now.'

'Puny human, the playground is off limits today. Anti-Cleanorist Squad is investigating.'

'This doesn't look like an investigation to me,' said Vedika. Redfly looked up as some of his comrades tittered.

'Buzz off before we take a big, juicy bite off you,' said Redfly, waving his goo-filled leg.

'Kab is not scared of you,' shouted Meera, standing next to me, hands on waist. Oh, she was so wrong. I was scared. Very, very scared. Wouldn't you be if you were faced with twisted, snarling garbage monsters?

'Show them the offering, Kabir!' said Dhruv. I sneaked behind Kungfu. Redfly eyed the cleanbot lazily.

'What is this?'

'A...uhm...' I tried. My mind went completely blank. Lila came on my side.

'It's a crap creator,' she said.

'A crap creator?' exclaimed Redfly. His grainy tongue flicked over his cake-covered lips. 'How does it work?'

'It can create rottenest, filthiest scum for you! Chocolate-flavoured.'

'Choco—' Redfly hummed around the cleanbot's body. His lips slobbered. 'As a Captain of Trash Rajah's formidable army, I command you to create the rottenest, filthiest, feces-filled chocolate cake!'

The cleanbot did nothing.

'Lies,' Redfly slobbered 'Humans always tell lies.'

'No!' said Lila. 'You've to show it a sample. Throw some cake at it.'

'I'm bored of this babbling human. Moustique—' Moustique was a starved-looking monsterquito, who till how had been splashing in a filthy pool. He looked up. '—weren't you just craving some blood? Bite her.' He fixed his steely eyes on Lila.

'We are not afraid of you, you blood-sucking brutes!' shouted Meera. 'We want our playground back!'

'Our killing machine will destroy you!' I screamed, waving my fist threateningly.

I *know*. Not my style but I was going with my team here. Being a hero is all about leading others. 'You and your garbage army will be smashed to smithereens!'

Redfly rolled in the rotten cake pile, tittering. 'You're entertaining,' he chuckled.

'Kungfu Cleanbot!' I shouted. Kungfu Aunty activated and hovered two inches from the muddy ground. 'I command you to destroy these garbage monsters!'

Kungfu Aunty's eyes glowed a calm white. She hovered. She kept hovering. She did nothing. No action. None. Nada.

'Robot! You have been ordered to attack!' I tried again.

The monsterquitoes tittered. They polished their sword beak with the dirty waters of the puddle. The mindbogglingly stubborn Kungfu bot remained stationary. It blinked once and kept hovering. No useful cleaning aids, no arms, not even an analysis.

'Move,' I pushed it in fury, 'you metallic freak! *Move*!' The robot's eyes deepened yellow before turning white. It stood still.

'Okay, enough,' said Redfly. 'I'm bored. Mous Dier, marinate these little creatures in our special dung drink!' He turned back into the pile of fruit cake, soaking himself into its soft, mushy gunk. Mous Dier, a bloatrat the size of a Great Dane, flicked to attention. He stood next to a dump. Noxious fumes came out of it. He signalled his buddies and they brought out broken buckets filling them with what looked like a nasty mix of goo and poo.

'Lila! Why is this hygiene pot not attacking?' I asked, inching away.

'That's what I was trying to tell you, Bhaiya,' said Lila, her tone cheerful. 'Kungfu Aunty told me she's a pacifist so she won't fight. She only cleans if its messy.'

'What's a pacifist?' frowned Meera.

'Aunty said it means she likes to stay away from violence. Like Gandhiji.'

'The monsterquitoes can have a go after they're soaked,' Redfly said. Attentive, mean-looking monsterquitoes rose up from the soaking puddles on the other side. They droned in our direction, following the bloatrats.

'What? You telling me this, *now*?' I said. The bloatrats had reached us with their special marinate.

'I suggest we sprint,' said Vedika.

Oh, well. I tried, right? I've been telling you since the beginning that I'm not really a hero, but I did try to fight for the playground. However, I am smart enough to recognize that one should stop being a hero when the alternative is being dead.

'Run!' I echoed. I grabbed Lila's hand, turned and tried to run.

Lila, being Lila, didn't move.

# A TRICKY PLAN

'Bhaiya, wait–'

'Now's not the time, Lila! Come!' I pulled her arm. The others had already started to move towards the exit gate. 'That maniac automaton will do nothing to help us!'

The bloatrats reached Kungfu and swung their buckets of poop. Lila squiggled from my grip and ran straight towards them. 'Lila!' I shouted, following her. My sister stood next to Kungfu as the bloatrats splashed the mucky brine they had brought onto both her and the pesky pacifist. A bloatrat pounced on Lila.

'No!' I screamed, jumping onto the beast. The monsterquitoes grabbed me, trying to pull me away.

'Get your filthy paws off my sister!' I cried, struggling with the bloatrat who had attacked Lila.

'Kungfu Aunty!' shouted Lila, struggling under the weight of the bloatrat. 'By the promise of Three Dragons, you need to clean up this mess!'

Dangling between four bloatrats, I whipped my face around. Through a cloud of fatflies that now hovered on top of me, I saw the robot's eyes turn a bloodied red.

**CONTAMINATION ASSESSMENT IN PROGRESS.**

A bloatrat grabbed my left foot. I kicked it. Two monsterquitoes pierced my oxyhelm, which dealt with them with a humming pleasure. Fatflies descended on the mucky grime that covered my oxysuit, licking it with pleasure.

**EXTREME CONTAMINATION DETECTED. PROCEDURE TO COMBAT CONTAMINATION IS AS FOLLOWING: PEST CONTROL. VIRULENT VIRUS SUPPRESSION. REGURGITATION OF FOOD WASTE AND BIODEGRADABLE MATERIALS. WASTE DECOMPOSING. DUST CONTROL. ION SCRUBBING.**

Besides me, Lila tussled with a monsterquito, screaming like a banshee. A timer started on Kungfu Aunty's smooth body. The monsterquitoes and bloatrats intensified their attack.

**01.15**
**01.14**
**01.13**

'The mad machine will wait for an hour!' I exclaimed. 'Lila, by that time, we will be in the hospital.'

I tumbled towards my sister, decided enough was enough. I was the elder, wiser sibling. 'We have to leave, Lila!'

Through the onslaught of the monsters, I grabbed my silly sister's hand. We staggered up and started to run, monsterquitoes, fatflies and bloatrats following us.

In the middle of the mayhem, Kungfu Aunty made a thin, keening noise.

'Wait,' said Lila, stopping fifty feet away from the gate. A rather enthusiastic bloatrat banged into my buttocks, trying to bite it through the oxysuit.

'Lila!' I tugged her hand. 'Please. Let's go!'

'Bhaiya! We have to help her. Bring out your weapons!'

I looked behind. Kungfu hovered mid-air, rotating like a ballet dancer in the middle of the playground. A pulsing light emitted from her. Multiple robotic arms shot out of her smooth body. One of the arms became a laser light. Another arm appeared with a microphone that emitted a sharp, ear-splitting sound.

*EeeeEeeeEeeeeEeee!*

I kicked a bloatrat off Lila's boot. Another pounced on my oxysuit, making me tumble. I struggled with its sharp teeth, as it growled and tried to bite my protected shoulder. I took the torch-like thing Lila had given me and rammed it up its throat.

Lila ran towards Kungfu, wielding her wand like a weapon. The bloatrat attacking me stiffened and fell off. Someone shooed the fatflies hovering on top of us like a grim cloud. Vedika. From the ground, I saw Meera following Lila.

I stood up. Attracted to the pulsating light that Kungfu emitted, garbage monsters started to circle her, leaving us alone. Monsterquitoes buzzed, bloatrats spiralled, fatflies buzzed rapturously.

'Stop this nefarious nonsense!' cried Redfly. His chariot lurched as the two dragonflies carrying him froze midair, hypnotized by the pulsating light. 'I command you to stop!'

A snout shot out of the top of Kungfu Aunty's smooth rectangular body. Her eyes became ruby, turning crimson, almost black.

'She's going for the Titanic Thwacks of Fuming Ferret, Bhaiya!'

A monsterquito jabbed Lila's oxysuit. She poked it with her wand.

The word that I usually uttered around Lila, which sounded very much like a confused 'wha?' was absorbed as Kungfu screamed.

Eeeeeeeeeaaaaaaah!

Spinning, faster and faster, she started to hammer the monsters.

*Swatswatswatswatswatswat....swat!*

She clobbered fatflies, smashed bloatrats, whacked monsterquitoes. It all became one big blur as monsters began to fall off the skies onto the ground, becoming bits of goo.

Some though, like Captain Redfly, were smart. They steered away from the attack, hiding behind burnt trees or started to head to the skies and the gate.

'Woah!' exclaimed Meera.

‘Everyone! We need to help Kungfu Aunty,’ said Lila. ‘Bring out the weapons she gave you.’

‘How does this work?’ shouted Vedika to be heard over the din.

‘Meera didi, you have the Citronella Atomizer. You focus on the monsterquitoes that are trying to escape.

‘Bhaiya, Vedika, use your Shaolin Sabers to cut down the bloatrats. Dhruv, aim the Woozy Wand into their eyes. It’ll make them fall asleep.’

‘What’s that in your hand?’ I cried.

‘Sonicbroom!’ smiled Lila, raising up what looked like a trumpet.

As the robot twirled and swirled, spouting ‘Eeeyah! Eeeyah!’, we also began to fight, using the weapons Lila had given us. I sluiced bloatrats with my saber. A little behind me, Meera weaved deftly through the puddles, aiming her Atomizer.

Meanwhile, new arms cropped out of the robot’s polished face. These ones had sprays.

‘That’s Citro Crane That Gobbles Pain!’ Lila shouted as she sent a blast of sonic-whatevery up in the skies.

‘Gobbles-*what*?’ I stared at my sister. Sometimes, dear reader, Lila can be quite obtuse. At that very moment, Kungfu’s hose sprayed the monsterquitoes. It was a thousand times more powerful than what Meera had.

*Fizzz. Fizzzz. Faaaaz. Fizzz. Faaaaaz.*

Monsterquitoes and fatflies rained around us, tumbling to the ground, snoring away. I hit one with my boot. Blood dribbled into the mud. Monsters were fluttering, winging, hopping, buzzing away. Two bloatrats saw my saber and scooted away.

‘Don’t you run!’ Redfly winged haphazardly over the scuttling bloatrats, a walkie-talkie in hand. His voice echoed through the playground, deafeningly. ‘Bring the missiles! Bring in the missiles!’

Ominous clouds darkened the grey skies. I looked up and panicked. Virulates and Particulators gusted in, attracted by the mayhem.

Particulators and Virulates were the deadliest of Trash Rajah's elite army. Made of nasty viruses and carbon particles, they infected human lungs, making it hard for us to breathe. Our oxyhelms and oxysuits could protect us from them, but they weren't a hundred per cent monster proof.

'Take cover!' I shouted.

'Wait, Bhaiya! I'll Sonicbroom,' Lila whipped out the trumpet and blew it into the skies. A disturbance erupted from her weapon, heading up into the carbon-laden monsters above.

Boom! They blasted, scattering into the skies. I watched agape, not moving even as I saw more monsterquitoes and fatflies flying in.

'Look!' cried Lila. Meera and Vedika turned to look to where Lila was pointing. 'Aunty's doing the Black Dragon Havoc. I programmed that into her.'

Kungfu Aunty popped out ten additional arms. She spun, zapped, struck, whipped, moving so fast, it made me dizzy. More monsterquitoes fell to the ground. Bloatrats piled on top of each other. Fatflies lay breathing hard. Virulates and Particulators vanished into the skies.

'Run, fly, scoot!' screamed Redfly, now without a chariot. He flew up into the sky, disappearing into the haze above. In a second, all monsters were gone.

We hollered in our excitement and fell onto the ground, exhausted. Kungfu wasn't done though. Four new arms rose out of her. She zoomed across the playground. One arm vacuumed and nano-scrubbed, another sopped up plastic and glass. The third sucked rotten trash, emitting it out as mulch, while a suction pump cleared potholes. She cleaned methodically, in grids.

Kungfu stopped exactly an hour later. She rolled back into a cuboid shape and halted next to Lila. On Lila's signal, Meera allowed others to enter the playground.

As children walked in, they gasped.

Their playground had been transformed. The ground was laid with grass, no broken glass, trash or plastic in sight. Flowerbeds had real flowers. Even the trees had been scrubbed clean. I could actually see the real colour of leaves for the first time in my life.

'Why did she paint the plants green?' squinted Tanay, crouching near a flowerbed.

'That's the original colour of plants, Tanay,' Vedika rolled her eyes.

'They're black, you silly. They've always been black.'

'No. They were black because of all the grime on them. Ask our hero.'

I smiled, ready to take all the praise of having brought the playground out of the monstrous grasp of Redfly and his minions.

'What do you say, Lila?' said Vedika. Wait. What was happening here?

'Lila, you're so brave!' cried Ishani, hugging her tight. 'Everyone, she's my brother's best friend. She even saved him from fatflies!'

Meera came and pulled me up. She slapped me on my back. 'You're so lucky, Kab. You have a superhero for a sister,' she said, awe in her voice.

'I want to be a monster hunter like you, Lila,' exclaimed Virat in a thin, excitable voice. He sounded like a baby! 'Please make me your pupil.'

'I also want to...'

'Our hero!'

Lila had indeed become famous. Everyone, including Sajan and Vivaan of the trashbomb team, gathered around Kungfu Aunty and Lila, sitting in a circle, facing them.

'There is more work to do. We will need to make a lot of biobins and use dustbins,' said Lila.

'Dustbins?' frowned Virat. 'Are they like the weapon you were holding?'

'No silly, it's a box where you put all your waste,' said Dhruv, elbowing his way in and sitting next to my sister. Lila nodded.

'My Mom wrote we should put rotten food, paper, plastic, and all other kinds of waste into the dustbin. She wrote if we don't feed the garbage monsters and dispose our trash carefully, the monsters will disappear.'

'Why do we need dustbins? Kungfu Aunty can fight the monsters like she did today,' said Meera.

'Aunty cannot always fight. Trash Rajah rules us because we need him to eat the garbage we produce. If we tackle our own trash, we don't need garbage monsters! Using dustbins is the only way.'

'No!' I shouted. Silence fell in the crowd. Everyone stared at me. 'Dustbins are *illegal.* Against the law.'

'So what,' shouted Ishani. 'I've had it with fatflies bullying me. I want dustbins!'

'Dealing with fatflies is one thing, but what Lila is saying is illegal. That's treason! We can get hurt,' I exclaimed.

'I want dustbins,' said Tanay.

'Me too.'

'Yes, us too. Why are you being like this, Kabir?'

'He's scared,' said Meera, softly. She looked at me disappointedly. I gulped. But this was important. They were talking like rebels.

'Hah! Kabir is a coward!' sneered Virat.

'Scared?' I shouted. 'Have you even thought of this? Your parents can get jailed. Or get hurt like my Mom did!' I stormed out of the playground, tears brimming in my eyes. Scared my foot. I will show the traitors!

# TIMES OF TRASH

## BEWARE CITIZENS!

### A MURDEROUS CLEANORIST IS ON THE LOOSE

Pretty City is under attack! A secret organization, by the name of TunfuTanty, led by a cleanorist has been seen attacking Trash Rajah's army. So far 2054 separate cases of assaults have been reported by the Bloatrat Police, Special Monsterquitoes Forces and the Fatfly Army.

The major impact has been on food sources for Trash Rajah's brave army. Evil Dustbins are appearing in all parts of the city, gobbling food, starving soldiers. 'Dustbins are banned for a good reason,' says Mr Junkfan, Rajah's prime secretary and the mayor of Pretty City. 'If evil dustbins take all the food that is meant for Rajah and his garbage army, our protectors will starve. Who will save us then? This cleanorist threatens our peaceful city's safety.'

So far two contingents of the army have been deployed to find those who are part of the TunfuTanty Army …

## RAJAH VAANI

### PRETTY PUBLIC SCHOOL PRINCIPAL TAKEN FOR CLEANORIST INTERROGATION

'The school authorities and our children have nothing to do with this cleaning attack!' cried Ms Ashraf, principal, Pretty Public School. 'Our management has already ordered fifty tons of top-quality human filth from the Holy Palace of Fume to desanitize our premises. We are a world-class facility of Trash Rajah's Pretty City and proud of it.' The authorities announced that Pretty Public School will be closed till further notice as investigations into the attack are progressing.

## TRASHISTAN TIMES

**Five dustbins spotted stealing food at the Royal Sump Kitchen**

# *The New Yuck Times*

## WE DON'T WANT ANYONE CONTROLLING OUR JUNK!

'We banned dustbins as they restricted our freedom. We have a right to throw human waste anywhere we like. On the streets, in our homes, in playgrounds and in lakes! It's true freedom that Trash 'Rajah and his generous army give us,' says Mayor Junkfan, The Mayor added that he's working closely with the Anti-Cleanorist Special Squad to find leads to the TunfuTanty Army. 'We will arrest TungfuTanty before Trash Rajah's birthday celebrations,' he said confidently.

# *ROTTEN GARBAGE EXPRESS*

## SCHOOLBOY CAUGHT TRYING TO FEED ROTTEN FOOD TO A DUSTBIN

Human Dhruv Gambhir, 7, was caught red-handed by Constable Tutt Bloatrat, trying to feed a rogue dustbin. By law, all rotten food is to be fed to Rajah's starving soldiers.

'I want to rid my city of vermin!' the boy shouted as the Bloatrats Police took him away for interrogation.

Principal Ashraf, the principal of Pretty Public School where Dhruv is a student, was visibly shaken. 'We can assure everyone that Dhruv was misled. We will do everything to help with the Anti-Cleanorist Special Squad investigation.'

## CURFEW TILL FURTHER NOTICE

By the Order of

### MAYOR JUNKFAN

*Special Member, Anti-Cleanorist Special Squad, Trash Rajah Army*

In the light of cleanorist activities, a curfew has been put in place immediately in all neighbourhoods of Pretty City. It's a step in human protection and security. We suggest all humans to remain at home in the week before Trash Rajah's birthday. Be good citizens! Produce more trash and feed Trash Rajah's starving soldiers. *Report any evil dustbins in your neighbourhood to 666-JUNK-FAN.*

# WHEN HOME COMES CRASHING DOWN

The Kungfu Aunty incident quickly spiralled out of control. Just like I had predicted. The cleanbot went missing. Police started to investigate. Thankfully Captain Redfly couldn't identify us as we were wearing oxysuits that day. But he arrested Principal Ashraf and closed the school down.

I hoped this was all there would be. That everyone would forget about the incident in a few days. We will produce trash and attend

Trash Rajah's birthday celebrations. I would play in the junior league finals.

But it didn't stop. Mysterious dustbins and biobins started to crop up in all parts of Pretty City. To my surprise, people—even sensible adults—started to feed trash to these dustbins. Overnight, there was no rotten food piling up in the middle of parks, no garbage on street corners. Trash Rajah's army started to starve. Just like Lila had wanted.

Why was everyone being so reckless? Why were people not following laws and rules? Were they not scared that they would be punished? Or worse, go missing like my Mom?

A week later, Pretty City went under curfew. Too many people were using dustbins and the authorities had to stop them. They increased policing in our streets. More people started to get arrested. The army and police were looking for Kungfu Aunty everywhere. Still, every day, new biobins kept appearing in street corners, in the parks, near people's homes.

Two days into the curfew, Dad put the school incident and Kungfu together. Not because I told him anything, but someone at work told him a story. They told him how a group of school kids had stood up against Rajah's army to get their playground. To support these heroes, all his colleagues had decided to use dustbins.

That evening, Dad put our dinner plates in front of us and eyed me.

'Tell. Me. *Everything*,' he said, his voice a whisper.

I did. Lila took my cue and told the truth. Instead of being angry with us, as I would have thought would happen, he was scared. Just like I was. He bolted all the doors and windows and went very, very silent, speaking softly.

'We need to find the cleanbot and destroy it,' he said.

'I agree,' I said.

'That would make Rajah's armies win, Dad!'

'We have no choice, Lila! After what happened to your Mom, I can't take a chance with both of you.'

'Don't do anything to Kungfu Aunty, please,' said Lila. She started to cry. Dad took Lila in his arms and hugged her as she sobbed.

'It's too late, sweetie,' he whispered softly. 'Rajah's armies are ruthless. They can destroy us. I...I can't have that! I want to protect you both. We need to find the cleanbot and destroy the lab.'

'You can't destroy Mom's lab!' I exclaimed.

'We have to, Kabir. Come with me.' He took my hand. We went upstairs.

Dad tucked Lila into bed. Kissed her. We went to the laboratory.

'Your Mom always had a fail-proof plan for her inventions,' he told me. 'There must be some kind of a controller, a remote, that can call the cleanbot back to the lab. She always had those for cleanbots.'

Dad sifted through various shelves, peeking behind things, scuffling, moving papers, peeping under tables. 'It could look like a game controller, with a couple of buttons.'

'Dad!' A vision of Lila showing something like a remote to Dhruv at school, swam in my mind. 'I think I know what—'

*Crassssssh!*

A thunderous noise made it feel like the ceiling had crashed. The walls of our home shook. I lurched. Dad grabbed me and ran back up.

*Crash! Boom! Crash!*

The living room was a complete mess. All windows and the door had been smashed in. A vile, foul smell leaked in, curling its smoky fingers around us. Virulates.

'Kabir! Go wear your oxysuit! And make sure Granny Gee and Lila wear theirs too.'

I blindly ran towards the closet in the corridor and banged into a shadow.

Hands clamped my shoulders. A bony man with clammy, botched skin. Bloatrats scuttled behind him, jabbering, grinning, wielding infecting weapons.

'Hello, there,' he smiled. His teeth were yellowed and stained and his body reeked. He patted my head. 'You've grown well.'

Dad stilled as if he had seen a ghost.

'Mister Randheer Singh.'

'Hello, Mayor Junkfan. This is rather late for a visit,' said Dad softly. Mayor Junkfan wore a torn brown tweed suit and a crumpled tie. He grinned, his eyes shining too bright. He didn't reply to Dad. Instead he walked around in our living room and picked up a copy of Wild Wuss.

'Ahh, Wild Wuss,' he said. 'He was my favourite hero when I was a boy. Such sensible advice.' Junkfan walked towards me and bent down. 'So, you read these?'

'Yes,' I said. Dad was standing behind the mayor, frozen.

'You should have told your Dad and Mom to follow Wild Wuss's advice. Never get into trouble if you want to live long.'

'Kabir,' Dad walked from behind the mayor and grabbed me. His fingers dug into my shoulders. He didn't look at me. Instead he said, 'Go to Granny's room with Lila. Whatever happens, *do not* come down.'

'But Dad—'

'No arguments, please!' said Dad, briefly making eye contact, before turning to face Mayor Junkfan. 'Can you explain why your team have broken into my house?'

Mayor Junkfan leered.

'Where are the others from your wife's cohort?'

'I have told you before. I do not know where her colleagues went after you betrayed them, Junkfan.'

My heart thundered. The person who had betrayed my mother to Trash Rajah had been Mayor Junkfan? My fingers curled into fists.

'It wasn't a betrayal. It was a sensible thing to do. Their rebellion would have failed. Just like yours. We have concrete information that the cleanorist has a connection to this family. Given your wife's activities, I'm not very surprised.'

My heart lurched. Did they find out? What will happen?

'We don't know anything.'

'And I don't believe you,' leered the mayor. He signalled a bloatrat. 'Mr Singh, you are being arrested for planning and leading a terror attack against Trash Rajah's innocent soldiers.' Bloatrats jumped onto my father, bringing him down onto the floor.

'No!' I shouted, running towards them. Two bloatrats grabbed me on either side, growling, their sharp teeth slobbering on my face.

'Don't fight! Protect your sister, Kabir!' cried Dad. Bloatrats jumbled around him, tying him up in fishnets.

'It was Kungfu! Not my Dad!' I shouted. Mayor Junkfan turned, crouched and stared at me, his face inches away from mine.

'Then bring me TunfuTanty,' he sneered, 'and I will set your father free.'

A grisly black cloud surrounded Dad. He gasped, invisible. Bloatrats pulled him out of the door into the dark night. I stared at the empty doorway and the crashed door.

Dad was gone.

# TRASH RAJAH'S LUNCH TIME

What happened next is something I'm not very proud of. However, it had to be done. To save Dad. Nothing else was important.

The morning after Dad was kidnapped, I left Lila with Granny and headed to Lila's room and found the controller, a small-sized remote.

Granny Gee made a vile concoction to protect us against pollution. I gulped down the bitter-sour potion without protest. When she took her nap, I sneaked out of the house.

The controller lay heavy in my pocket as I began to walk on the dirt road that led to

Lethal Lake—the biggest lake in the middle of the city, and a greasy, dense mulch, infested by plastocrocs and oiliguanas.

In the middle of the lake was Puke Peak, a mountain-sized island made of garbage. On the top of this peak was Supremely Vile Stadium. Towering above the stadium was Trash Rajah's personal residence, Palace of Fume.

I took the rickety bridge made of concrete and rubble, that led from the banks of Lethal Lake to the island in the middle. Preparations for Trash Rajah's birthday were already underway.

Monsterquitoes and fatflies hurried back and forth on the pathway that led to the Puke Peak island, bringing trash in buckets and troughs from the mainland for the massive treat two days later.

The planks groaned under my feet, sometimes dipping into the oily surface of the lake. A plastocroc floated near me, eyeing my movements lazily. It opened its jaws, showing a vast plastic mouth that could suffocate me with a bite. I hurried.

The Puke Peak island was surrounded by a mushy sump. A contingent of monsterquitoes tittered as I walked to the path leading up the mountain. One of them pricked my oxysuit. I held my breath, hoping it hadn't pierced all the way through. I trudged along the pathway, weaving around broken pieces of furniture, toys, gadgets and other human trash.

Out of breath, I finally reached Supremely Vile Stadium, a large stadium on top of the plateaued Puke Peak. The stadium bustled with preparation. In two days, all citizens of Pretty City would be here, cheering for their king. I had always attended these birthday celebrations with my family. This year, I was supposed to compete in the junior league. Today though, trashball felt like such a distant dream.

Behind the stadium and above it, loomed the Palace of Fume. It was a leaning tall tower made of rubble. Bricks, stones, coal, boulders, steel rods, cement bits from destroyed human buildings had been piled up together. The palace rose up into the skies, to create a fifty-storey-high structure. Since it was rubble and debris, the building heated up and always attracted a nest of Particulators that liked to swim around it.

Legend had it that no human, except for Mayor Junkfan, had ever entered the palace and returned. I stopped in front of its rusted gate.

'Where do you go, little human,' growled a guard. It was a dogroach, a mean, massive-sized hybrid canine which had a compound eye and antennas like a cockroach, but also a nasty, biting tendency. Dogroaches were part of Trash Rajah's personal guard.

I gulped. Its compound eye stared at me, reflecting my panicked face. Fat drops of acidic spit hung from its massive mouth. A single drop of it could burn through my oxysuit.

'I...I'm here to meet Mayor Junkfan. I have information about the cleanorist...'

The dogroach snarled. I staggered back. This was it. My end. All thanks to my sister. He spat into a mike that sizzled, stopped, heard as someone else spoke. A moment later, the gates opened.

'Little human,' he growled, 'the mayor is with Trash Rajah in his chamber on the top floor. Zigzag up the Scuttle stairs—' he nodded to a doorway with rickety stairs—'and enter the door after the Mantle of Mottled Molasses.'

'What's the Mantle of Mottled Molasses?' I asked.

'The prettiest artwork in the world.' The canine roach's antenna quivered in ecstasy.

The tower rose up into the grey haze above, becoming invisible. I gulped, wondering if I should follow my hero Wild Wuss and just give up. *Want to live longer? Stay out of trouble.*

The dogroach snarled. I hurried towards the stairway and started to climb up. The stairs circled around the tower.

It reeked. Like hundreds of unflushed toilet bowls stacked together. The stench leaked even through the protective oxysuit, making me nauseous. I gagged, but kept climbing. The walls and the stairs were dangerous. Things stuck out of them. A broken table's leg. A smashed TV. Twisted and blackened mesh of steel. Weathered wall of a bedroom. My heart skipped a beat as I walked around a carcass of a deer.

My oxysuit had become hot inside. My palms were sweaty. Wild Wuss would have never come to Puke Peak. No matter what. He would have stayed out of trouble. But what choice did I have?

'Focus,' I said to myself. I had to save Dad.

After climbing up and up for what seemed like hours, I reached a landing which smelled of vomit-flavoured ice-cream. A massive fountain covered a whole wall. Rotten treacle dripped from its ceiling towards a collecting pool below. Millions of worms and tiny slugs wriggled in it, building ridges and caverns, swimming.

This definitely looked like the Mantle of Mottled Molasses. I located a door beside it, nodded to another dogroach who stood guard there and stepped in.

A dark, damp tunnel that looked like an intestine led me deep into the palace. This was fast becoming a bad, bad idea.

The far end of the dank corridor opened into a cavern, with roughly carved walls made of debris, cement, steel, bricks and bits of broken buildings. The high walls ended jagged, steel rods rising up in the skies. A heavy population of Particulators and Virulators swam above in the skies, blocking the sun.

In the middle of the cavern was a ridge of squelchy stuff, like a giant worm of rotten food. A colossal, gooey collation of all kinds of refuse.

I started to walk around it, trying to locate Mayor Junkfan.

'Mayor?' I called, my voice trembling. The mound moved. Up and down. Breathed. It was a creature. Alive. Sprawled across the vast floor of the cavern, tentacles erupting from it.

In between the circle of tentacles, was a giant mouth, with fat lips. At first, I didn't recognize it. Trash Rajah had changed so much since I'd last seen him—a year ago, on his last birthday. He had deformed, and expanded into a giant worm.

We had been taught that to protect humans, Trash Rajah had started to consume the trash we created. But there was so much trash, that he couldn't do it alone and so garbage monsters were born.

I looked at the giant before me and could not find a trace of anything human—a face or eyes or legs. All I could see was a big, round, black hole of a mouth. A bottomless pit, held together by greyed lips. The mouth was the size of two trucks side to side. He opened his mouth. A black tongue wriggled out of it.

From my left emerged Mayor Junkfan who signalled eight monsterquitoes that dragged a plate upto Trash Rajah's vast mouth. Rajah's lips gobbled the plate, the food and the eight monsterquitoes. The lips closed, before opening again.

'More,' he rumbled. His blackened tongue slobbered.

'This is all there is today, Your Highness of Terrible Trash.'

'Does Pretty City want us to starve?' hollered Trash Rajah. The floor shook, the patched-up walls rattled with displeasure. I moved quickly as monsterquitoes and fatflies flew out of the cavern into the tunnel, trying to escape their king's wrath.

'You will get a massive feast on your birthday in two days, Highland Owner of all Garbage and of Human Feces,' said Mayor Junkfan.

'We want more. NOW!' His vast mouth opened. His slobbering tongue flicked up into the skies, catching a few Particulators. The rest flew away from his reach.

'There is nothing left, Terrible Tales of Trash,' Junkfan trembled, 'The cleanorist TunfuTanty likes to...pardon my language...but it likes to *clean*.'

'Clean?' Trash Rajah shuddered. 'Captain Redfly!' The walls shook dangerously. Captain Redfly popped from behind a column and quickly wiped chocolate goo from his face. 'Why hasn't the cleanorist been caught and drowned in Lethal Lake?'

Captain Redfly flew upwards, his golden filigree armour glinting. 'Mayor Junkfan has not helped in our investigations.'

'I haven't helped?' cried Mayor Junkfan. He shook in anger. 'I'm the one who gave you Randheer Singh!'

'Only a spouse to the scientist who we have dealt with seven years ago! Not the cleanorist. I saw it with my own eyes, O King of Terrible Trash! It's evil incarnated. It destroys soldiers, consumes trash. Even humans support the wretched terrorist.'

'That's not true!' cried Mayor Junkfan. 'All citizens are loyally working overtime to create more garbage so you can feed, Wise Ruler of Mount Potty.'

'Find this cleanorist!' hollered the king. A bomb of spit left his lips, smattering on a wall beside me. I jumped laterally, as the wall sizzled with acid.

'It's not that easy, Your High Mess,' said Captain Redfly. 'The cleanorist is hiding. It has also unleashed hundreds of dustbins onto Pretty City.'

‘Dustbins?’ squeaked Rajah. He lips noodled with wrath. ‘Dustbins are rot-eaters! They are toxic, evil, anti-national. Tell my armies to destroy them all. Find the cleanorist!’

‘I....’ I gulped, spoke louder. ‘I *know* where the cleanorist is...’

Junkfan and Redfly turned to see me. Redfly flew towards me.

‘You are Singh’s boy,’ said Junkfan.

‘Yes, Mr Mayor.’

‘You found this cleanorist?’

‘I...’ I gulped, clutching the controller behind my back, ‘I can bring Kungfu here. But, my Dad ...he doesn’t know anything. Please release him. You promised!’

Junkfan leered. He walked closer, towered above me. He smiled through his oxysuit. ‘Of course,’ he said, his lips becoming thin. ‘Captain Redfly, if you will?’

Redfly signalled to two dogroaches who stood in a corner on the other side. They darted across the cavern, through the tunnel out of the doors. A little later they came back again, dragging Dad who was bound in a fishnet.

'Dad!' I ran to him, 'Are you okay?'

'Kabir?' he said weakly, getting on his knees. His oxysuit was smashed and blood crusted his forehead. 'What are you doing here?'

'I've come to take you home.'

'Leave, Kabir! You cannot give the cleanbot to them!'

'I knew you had the cleanorist,' shouted Mayor Junkfan. 'Boy, if you want your father to live, be sensible like Wild Wuss and give me the cleanorist.'

There was no doubt in my mind. I brought out the controller, and pressed the calling button, hoping the signal would reach Kungfu cleanbot wherever she was. Nothing happened for a few moments.

Then suddenly a lightning flash lit up the skies. Virulates congealed above us, became bright purple, attracted to the pulsing light. The light flashed and the Virulates were torn to smithereens. Their bits rained into the cavern, and Kungfu Aunty descended from the skies above Trash Rajah. Her body glistened, squeaky clean, making the cavern look even more filthy in comparison.

Her eyes became beams of black lasers as she scanned the cavern and the lump we called our king.

**CONTAMINATION ASSESSMENT IN PROGRESS.**

'The cleanorist will kill our king!' shouted Captain Redfly. 'Stop it! Guards! Guards!'

I looked down at the controller and hesitated. Sighed. I pressed the Shut Down button.

**EXTREME CONTAMINATION DETECTED.**
**PROCEDURE TO COMBAT–**

The cleanbot stopped, hovered for a split second before it crashed onto the floor of the cavern with a soft splat sound. Her rectangular body lay like other machines that were part of the rubble around us. Dogroaches rushed and pounced on its still form, binding its cuboid body with fishnets and spit and goo. Captain Redfly hovered above it, snorting excitedly.

'We have caught the evil creature, O King of all Unclean Kings!' cried Junkfan.

I quickly pocketed the controller.

'You have the cleanorist,' I said aloud, not looking in the direction of where Kungfu lay inert. 'Now release my father.'

Junkfan signaled the dogroaches holding my father. They started to unbind the fishnet.

'No,' rumbled Trash Rajah. Everyone froze, looking at their king. 'The cleanorist attacked us. It made us starve. The scientist who created the cleanorist will die! Both will be destroyed together.'

'But...but my father has nothing to do with *that*! He didn't create Kungfu cleanbot,' I cried.

'My Lord of Gentle Farts,' said Junkfan. He walked to the middle of the cavern to face the giant lips. 'Generosity suits someone of your Grand Stature. You are the protector of our people. We should release innocent citizens.'

'We will show Pretty City who is king!' hollered Trash Rajah. Missiles of spittle spun from his lips into all direction. Junkfan rolled, narrowly avoiding one spit. 'We have been too kind, too generous. We will destroy the cleanorist and the scientist together on our birthday. Our decision stands.' Trash Rajah rumbled. The floor shook.

Two dogroaches pounced on my father, rolling him up in fishnets. Captain Redfly glinted triumphantly above them.

'Dad!' I ran. Someone grabbed my oxysuit. Junkfan turned me, face to face.

'You promised!' I shouted. 'He's *innocent*!'

'It's been decided by the king,' said Junkfan. 'Remember what Wild Wuss says? Keep away from a fight.'

Dad was dragged by the snarling guards out of the cavern.

'Dad!' I tried to pry myself out of Junkfan's grip.

'You need to leave,' cried Junkfan. His eyes were filled with fear. 'Before you die.'

'But...my father,' I said. Trash Rajah's fat belly rumbled.

'Now. *Leave*!'

My heart lurched, but I turned and started to run across the dark corridor. The doors slammed shut behind me as I started to spiral down the palace stairs.

Trash Rajah was gone. As was my father.

# LILA HAS A BACKUP

I ran and ran till I reached home. I didn't know what to do. Taking off my oxysuit, I crumbled in the disinfection vestibule, sobbing.

My hands shook. My body shook. I had failed. Miserably. But why? When I had given the forsaken cleanbot to them, why hadn't they released my father? Why had Trash Rajah decided to punish my father for doing the lawful thing? Someone opened the vestibule door.

'Not now, Granny!' I screamed, hitting the door with a shoe.

'Bhaiya...' the door opened further and Lila peeped in. 'Why didn't you get Dad from Rajah's palace?'

I frowned.

'How did you know I had gone there?'

Lila made a face.

'You stink of Lethal Lake. And I saw you took the controller. I thought you've gone to fight Trash Rajah.'

I got up and walked into the living room, feeling utterly miserable. My stomach felt heavy and I felt ill. It was time to own up the truth.

'I...I gave your Kungfu Aunty to Trash Rajah.'

'Good!' exclaimed Lila. 'She will clean him up!'

'No, Lila,' I said, 'I...I switched her off before I had her arrested. The cleanbot will be...*Aunty* will be destroyed on Trash Rajah's birthday.'

'Oh.'

'I wanted to protect Dad. I thought they will give him back to us if I gave them Kungfu Aunty but...they didn't. I failed.' I fell on the sofa and sobbed. 'I failed. I'm so sorry.'

Something moved by my side. I looked up. Lila snuggled besides me, stroking my hair.

'I'm sorry too, Bhaiya. You were right. We put Dad in trouble by standing up against the garbage army. I got us all into trouble.'

I sat up and hugged my sister. 'No! You were right! I thought if we follow the laws, we will be safe. But it's not true. Trash Rajah and his minions *are* bullies. They don't want to set Dad free, even though he's innocent. Trash Rajah wants to punish him to make us fear him. But I don't know what to do! How do we save Dad?'

Lila twiddled her hands and pulled back, getting up on her knees on the sofa.

'Well, I have a plan to rescue Dad,' she said, smiling triumphantly.

'Dad's stuck in Trash Rajah's giant palace with dogroaches and whatnots protecting him. How can we rescue him?'

'Do you still have the controller?' she asked.

'What? Oh that? Yes.' I fished the remote out of my pocket. 'You can't do anything with it, Lila. Kungfu Aunty is switched off. This one cannot turn it back on.'

She smiled, lopsided, the way she did when she was thinking of something really, really twisted. I frowned. She got up, and beckoned me to follow her.

'You better tell me your whole plan,' I said, half running as we started to climb the stairs.

'We will attend Trash Rajah's birthday—'

'I'm never going back to that hell again!' I cried.

She stopped, turned and said matter-of-factly, 'and *destroy* him and his garbage monsters.'

I tripped on the next step. Where did my sister get all these ideas from?

'Are you *mad*? That's impossible. Do you know how many soldiers Trash Rajah has? He has an army!'

'And we have a smart plan, Bhaiya.' Lila's eyes glinted, much like Kungfu Aunty's would when she was about to clean. 'A lot of us.'

'Who else have you brought into your plan?'

'There's Kungfu Aunty, you and some of our school,' she smiled.

Being Lila, she didn't tell me all at once. Instead, the next morning, after the curfew was lifted, she called a secret meeting at the gym hall in our school. There were twenty-five of us. All kids.

It was a mad, crazy plan, something only Lila could have thought possible. But then, my way the Wild Wuss way, had not worked. We had to do the impossible. We had to fight to protect ourselves. For this time, Trash Rajah had gone too far.

I decided to follow my sister's plan. I decided to do the brave thing.

To be a hero.

What a horrid idea.

# A TERRIBLE TREACLE TREAT

It was Trash Rajah's birthday. It was the biggest annual festival for Pretty City. No one could miss it. Trash Rajah had made it a law to attend. Anyone found not attending would be thrown into Lethal Lake.

A long line of monsters and humans snaked onto the bridge that led to Supremely Vile Stadium. Streamers made of cans, broken tubelights, smashed phones and keyboards hung like canopies above. Everyone carried boxes, bags, bottles of treats for the Rajah. Offerings you had to take. It was the law.

I stopped at the beginning of the pathway, my heart sinking as I remembered walking the same path two days ago. My throat felt dry.

'Are you sure it's going to work?' I whispered.

'Yes,' said Lila, taking my hand. 'You just focus on playing your game and I'll do the rest.'

'Hurry, hurry.' said Granny Gee, hitting me with her support cane. I staggered onwards, repositioning my heavy backpack.

A group of bloatrats, drunk on rotten cola, smashed bottles on the pathway, throwing them into the lake. Plastocrocs, swimming in the mucky lake, snapped at them. One of them threw a particulate bomb into the lake. It boomed, spreading muck, shaking the planks.

A little further away, Lethal Lake lit up in the purple fire of noxious firecrackers. Smoke curled up and swam towards us. We would have choked if it weren't for our oxysuits. How could the monsters be so unfair? Didn't they care about us at all?

'You're holding my hand too tight, Bhaiya,' said Lila. I loosened my grip, taking a deep breath. The line inched forward.

It took us an hour to reach the entrance of the stadium. Ten dogroaches growled at us, their compound eyes staring at each of the visitors.

'Offerings,' one snarled. I pushed out the concoction of Ayurvedic leftovers and toilet waste that we had brewed overnight. The guard eyed it through broken spectacles.

'What's this?'

'Odious Ayurvedic Fart Tonic,' said Lila.

'Odious Tonic, eh?' said the dograoch, antennas moving excitedly. 'Smells like Hell!'

'Yes!' said Lila. 'It's made of the best ingredients ever. We did a special all-night potluck at Pretty Public School to make this. Trash Rajah will burst with delight!'

The dogroach's antennas danced in pleasurable circles.

'Trash Rajah deserves loyal citizens like you,' he said. He pointed at a big opening of a drain behind him. 'Put it here.'

'Let me put some tonic at the other side too,' I said, moving across the gate in front of a monsterquito family. I dumped some of the vile decoction into the drain opening on the other side.

'Just two milliliter of human blood?' shouted a dogroach behind me. It was talking to the monsterquito and its family behind me. 'We will see what the Tribunal has to say about the love you show to our king.'

'Human blood is hard to get nowadays, sire. I have a big family,' said the monsterquito.

'In that case show your loyalty by making yourself the offering,' the dogroach snarled.

The monsterquito wailed as two dogroaches grabbed him, vanishing through a side passage.

'Okay. Next!'

Breathing again, I headed back towards Lila and Granny and walked in fast.

The two drains moved on either side of the stadium's seating area, like moats between the play area and the seats. The drains connected with each other in the middle of the stadium, which was a big sump of vomitous viscous slop. All offerings by all citizens were going to fatten this overflow.

Trash Rajah's Terrible Treacle Treat.

The ground itself was made of layers on layers of flattened discards—plastic, metal, aluminum, concrete, glass and other human wastes.

All humans sat on one side of the stadium, wearing oxysuits. All monsters and Trash Rajah's soldiers sat on the other side. Between our seating areas was the Palace of Fume on one side and a cliff on the other. The cliff gave a view of Lethal Lake and Pretty City behind it. A terrible reek wafted in from there, along with purplish fumes probably from particulate bombs thrown in by revellers.

I pulled Lila aside.

'You're sure this will work?' I whispered furiously.

'Granny gave me the recipe, Bhaiya.'

'She's a bit loony you know! It's Dad we're talking about.' She gave me a lopsided smile. Full of hope and optimism. I sighed. 'Just don't vanish from my sight.'

Lila nodded and took Granny up the stairs. I went down towards the bench where the Pretty Public trashball team was and sat next to Meera.

She held my gloved hand and squeezed it, smiling.

'All good?' I asked.

'Yes! All of us have added Rapid Rot to the Terrible Treacle. I'm glad you're a hero, Kabir.'

'Being a hero is overrated,' I mumbled, looking at Mayor Junkfan who had just entered the arena. Today he wore a bright red suit, crumpled, dirtied and torn. He dangled his mike, sending a smile my way. 'But sometimes we don't have a choice.'

Lila's miraculous plan all depended on Rapid Rot. Lila had found the recipe in Mom's diary. It was a potion that could instantly decompose rotten stuff. The ingredients hadn't been easy to find. Some of them Granny had helped with. The harder things had been earthworms and millipedes and fungi, for which we had taken the help of Gardener Kaka. We had made the sump together at Pretty Public School's gym hall. It had taken two days and nights to prepare it. Principal Ashraf and other teachers and parents had found out about it, but instead of stopping us, had helped. All of them were angry at how Rajah had given Dad a death sentence.

There was nothing to do now, except *wait*. And hope.

As humans and monsters settled in, noise and smoke filled the stadium. Lethal Lake burnt with noxious crackers. A wafting, stinky rotten-egg smell hung in the air. The skies were laden with coils of Particulators, their thick smoke curling about the humans, trying to find cracked oxysuits and lungs to infect.

A moment later, the stadium shook. Silence washed over us all. A whirlpool formed near Terrible Treacle. A jelly-like substance oozed out. It kept rising, like a black bubble of oil, becoming the size of a small hill.

The jelly giant had bits and pieces and things stuck in its gelatinous belly. It burped. Noxious fumes flew out of its crater-like vast mouth.

Trash Rajah was here.

'Ladies and gentlemen, I present to you, the Kindly Kingpin of Trash!' Junkfan shouted in the mike.

Humans cheered, hooted, clapped. Monstersquitoes tittered. Fatflies buzzed. Plastocrocs snapped their plastic-filled gums. Bloatrats squeaked. Dogroaches howled.

Rajah's cavernous mouth slobbered onto the Terrible Treacle Treat, his mandibles sucking, tentacles pulling in solids from the treat into his endless mouth. He guzzled, finishing it up in one hungry gulp.

It was too much food, even for him. His stomach rumbled.

'Oh, it's happening,' exclaimed Meera. I nodded, my heart drumming. Will he explode? He bloated and bloated.

A big, fat burp thundered out, sending a few monsterquitoes spiraling towards the cliff and into Lethal Lake. Eighteen little newborn Virulates rose up into the evening skies of Pretty City. Trash Rajah gargled in pleasure.

'More!' Trash Rajah thundered. Minions scurried towards him, dumping more food into his vast mouth.

'And now, for this evening's main show. The public destruction of cleanorists!' shouted

Junkfan. As if on cue, Trash Rajah puked sludge all across the ground.

'Ugh!' the mayor cried, looked up at his king. He quickly changed his sentence. 'I mean thank you for your kind approval, O Vast Mountain of Hope!'

'They don't expect us to play in *that mucky mulch*,' whispered Meera.

'Why hasn't he exploded,' I whispered, frowning. Rapid Rot had been successfully tried in Mom's lab. Could it be that it wouldn't work on Trash Rajah, who was so big? Could it decompose all the garbage that made Trash King?

I craned my neck to look for Lila but couldn't spot her.

'Wasn't that absolutely brilliant! To celebrate our generous and kind Trash Rajah's regime, we have a special programme for all of you,' Junkfan clapped his hands.

A row of dogroaches marched into the stadium, holding shiny pieces of twisted metal. The crowd—both humans and monsters—booed. It was Kungfu Aunty and her biobins. The bodies had been twisted and rolled into meshes. That wasn't all.

Two dogroaches pulled in a cart.

'Dad!' I cried. He was sitting inside, his oxysuit dirty and dented, a fishnet all around him. He looked pale, but otherwise unhurt. I ran towards him, or rather tried to. A hand clamped on him.

'Not now,' hissed Principal Ashraf, who had been standing beside the team. 'You have to play, Kabir.'

Dad spotted me . 'Where's Lila?' he shouted. I flipped around, to point him towards Granny and Lila. But Lila wasn't sitting next to Granny.

'Granny,' I shouted from across the rows of people, 'where's Lila?' Granny Gee grinned and waved her stick back at me.

'Kabir!' hissed Principal Ashraf. '*Sit*.'

A rumble sounded at the far end of the stadium drowning my voice. I sat back, staring at Dad. He was surrounded by dogroaches, still under arrest. A scourge of monsterquitoes flew up into the sky, pulling Kungfu Aunty and the biobins up.

'A surprise!' announced Junkfan. He raised his hands and exclaimed. 'Trash Rajah has devised a new game in his honour.'

Junkfan signalled to the monsterquitoes who took Kungfu Aunty and the biobins to the cliff side of the stadium. Multiple raised concrete pillars had been planted goal side, that jutted out like remains of an unfinished building. The biobins and Kungfu were tied to pillars with rusted chains. One push and they would plunge down into the lake.

'Our usual trashball contest is cancelled. We have a special treat for the Best Day of the Year. Trashbomb the Cleanorist!'

The stadium filled with claps and woofs and whistles and shrills. He waited for it to die down.

'The biggest shot on the cleanorists will receive a prize,' he screamed. 'A year's supply of worm-ridden chocolate cakes.'

'Oh, no,' I moaned. Worm-ridden chocolate cakes were the absolute favourite of all garbage monsters of any kind.

The monsters cheered. They began to fly, crawl, scuttle and pounce. They all headed towards the ground, to figure out what they could throw. Some tried to scoop bits of Trash Rajah's gloop. If Lila had a plan to save our Dad *and* her dear aunty, she had to do something *now*.

'Now?' asked Meera.

'Wait,' I said. 'We need Lila—'

But where was Lila? How would she signal us?

The monsters swarmed into the grounds, rolling, digging the stadium for rotten leftovers from Terrible Treacle Treat. They rolled them in the mulch, ferociously making tight balls of trashbombs.

Mayor Junkfan headed towards our sheltered booth as the monsters took over the grounds. He shook hands with Principal Ashraf.

'You can send the trashball team home. There will be no tournament this year,' he said. 'Wait—' he frowned looking at the other end of the ground. '—is that a girl?'

A human girl was climbing the pillar on which Kungfu Aunty was tied. I stared in disbelief. It was Lila.

'What is she doing?' I got up but was pulled back down. Meera gripped my oxysuit.

'Catch the little traitor!' screamed Junkfan. He ran towards the goalposts. Dogroaches leaped ahead of him, heading to the column where Lila stood. Monsterquitoes flew in her direction.

'She's switching her on. That's our signal!'

Meera called out to the trashball team and started to run into the ground, the team spreading in all directions. All of my team headed straight into the monster mob that surrounded Kungfu Aunty and the biobins.

'What's your trashball team doing?' cried Junkfan from behind.

'Participating, Mayor Junkfan,' smiled Principal Ashraf.

I stood frozen. Scared. I wanted to run away, but how could I? Lila had reached the robot. She climbed up the column like a monkey, and struggled around Kungfu, her little body dangling on the pole.

'Come Kabir!' cried Meera. Lila flicked the switch. Kungfu Aunty's eyes turned red. A deep, deep dark red. Almost black.

Kungfu Aunty broke the rusted chains with one tug. She rose up. Her varied arms spouted and squiggled.

**OVERWHELMING DATA. CIRCUITS OVERHEATING. ANALYSIS IN PROGRESS.**

'Stop the girl!' shouted Junkfan. Hordes of garbage monsters were already climbing the goalpost. Two monsterquitoes and fatflies pulled at Lila. Kungfu Aunty shoved Lila into her body.

'Now!' shouted Meera. We stood between the goal and the monsters, swung out the different weapons we had been hiding in our oxysuits. Shaolin Sabers for dogroaches. Citronella Atomizers for monsterquitoes. Stun Jabs to slow down and freeze monsters. Woozy Wand to make them sleepy.

'Long live Kungfu Army!' Virat shouted.

Zuuuup! Zuuuup! Zrrrrrr. Zrrrr. Psst! Shharp!

The garbage monsters didn't know what hit them. Our inventions spurted cleaning agents that stung and splayed the monsters and sent them scattering. My oxyhelm spouted needles. I head-butted a dogroach that tried to pounce at me.

'We are under attack!' shouted Junkfan. Trash Rajah rumbled with displeasure. His moans boiled nastily. People panicked and tumbled down the stadium stairs, heading towards exits. A few humans joined us in the fight against garbage monsters. Most scooted. Snarling dogroaches blocked the entrances.

'No one leaves till we capture the rebels!' hollered Captain Redfly. He entered in a brand-new chariot, flashing red bulbs. 'Grab the rebels!' he tinned.

I danced with my Shaolin Saber, grabbing Dhruv and cutting the dogroach that attacked him. Where was Kungfu Aunty? Why wasn't she helping? I handed over the injured boy to Principal Ashraf, turning around. The biobins were still tied to the columns. Kungfu Aunty was missing with Lila. Both of them had done a Vanishing Act.

A contingent of monsterquitoes plummeted down upon us. Bloatrats squeaked, dashing in our direction. Particulators and Virulates clouded around us, their porous tentacles trying to find an entry into our oxysuits.

The Kungfu Army was surrounded. We desperately needed help.

A bloodcurdling scream echoed through the stadium. Twisting mid-fight, I saw Junkfan, squiggling to keep a hold on something. A small body. Lila. A menacing dogroach inched towards her, his acid-filled mouth drooling.

'Stop all of you, or I'll feed her to the dogroa—aah!' he shouted. Lila had just whacked his oxyhelm off his head. She ran.

'Protect Lila!' I howled at Meera, jumping into a gang of bloatrats. Meera was the fastest runner in the team. She was the only one who could save Lila.

Meera ran towards my sister, grabbed her and rolled away. I swatted the fatflies that followed them, sending my saber into the mouth of a snarling dogroach.

In the middle of the stadium, Trash Rajah bloated up, furious. 'I'm sorry, Lord of Gluttony,' screamed Mayor Junkfan into the mike. 'I'm really sorry that your birthday—'

'Put the scientist on the last column,' said Trash Rajah. He burped. Two Virulates emerged from his mouth and released into the skies.

'No!' I shouted as five bloatrats pounced on me. Captain Redfly hovered triumphantly on top of Dad. Two snarling dogroaches flanked him.

Most of the team had been captured by Rajah's soldiers. On Junkfan's signal, dogroaches forced the audience back into their seats. Two others dragged Dad up the cliff on the other side of the stadium and tied him up on a column at the precipice of the cliff. His legs and arms dangled dangerously. He looked down and screamed. Plastocrocs and oiliquanas waited in the lake below, their oily mouths wide open in anticipation.

I finally spotted Trash Rajah's squinty eyes, hidden under folds of decadent flesh above his vast lips. They gleamed with hatred. 'Let the games begin.'

Junkfan towered over me, clamping his iron hand on my shoulder. 'Ready to save your father, Kabir?' he asked, smiling menacingly.

# LILA GOES MISSING. AGAIN.

The umpteenth trashbomb plummets in Dad's direction. Standing on the cliff, I lunge, headbutting it with my oxyhelm. Panting, I curse the day I had decided to follow Lila's mad plan.

You know the story now. Don't you agree with me? Kungfu Aunty is to blame for all our troubles. Instead of protecting Dad or helping us, she has vanished. Lila and Meera are missing too.

The rest of the trashball team have been arrested. They watch helplessly as Trash Rajah and his monster army play with me. I am all that stands between those trashbombs that zoom towards my Dad. Me and Mom's psycho oxyhelm.

And the garbage monsters are super motivated. They all really, really love worm-ridden rotten chocolate cakes. They will kill for even a bite. A year's supply means that the trashbombs have become bigger, meaner, more frequent and lethal. A couple of them have already sneaked through my barriers hitting Dad's oxysuit. The last one almost made him tumble into the lake.

I peek at Dad between trashbombs, gulping. He looks exhausted. And then there—a trashbomb whizzes by my right and hits Dad square on his oxyhelm. The rusted chains that hold him jangle and become loose. He falls a few feet, grabs a chain by his hand. I panic.

But wait, did it smell....nice? Has my smell sense gone bonkers? The trashbomb that whizzed past me and hit Dad smelt of lavender.

'No!' I cry. Only this time it's a jubilant one. Lila has done it again. A trashbomb hits me in the chest. I sniff. Oh, definitely lavender. I laugh.

A couple of trashbombs whizz past me, heading to Dad. They hit him softly, like feathers.

'Hold on, Dad!' I cry, look in the opposite direction. Someone snatches Junkfan's mike and runs.

'Kungfu Aunty do it!' Lila shouts. Her voice echoes through the stadium.

A metallic blur shoots across the sky. My head turns to see as Kungfu Aunty bolts into Trash Rajah's open mouth. She vanishes inside the cavern that is his mouth. A split second later, she comes back out, flying away.

The ground grumbles. Rajah's vast spread starts to bloat and bubble. The Rapid Rot! Kungfu Aunty has hurried the process of decomposing. She has added the last ingredient into it. Lavender.

The trashbombers turn their attention away from my father. They scuttle to their king who turns yellow and blue.

I scramble up.

'Dad!'

I can't see him on the ledge on top of the column anymore. My heart sinks. I run to the edge of the cliff, look down. Did he fall?

'Dad!' I call out.

'Kabir!'

I look up again, see Dad holding on to the ledge on the other side, legs dangling.

'Are you okay, Kabir?' he shouts. I roll my eyes. With Virat's help, I bring Dad down from the column.

Kungfu Aunty's busy with her Shaolin Saber that chops off the distracted monsters at 1000x the speed than mine. The others from the school have joined too. As have some human adults. After all, it's a fight for us all.

'Catch the cleanorist!' Redfly's voice booms.

No one heeds him. The garbage army stare at their king, who doesn't look good at all. I mean he was ill-looking to begin with, but now he looks decidedly horrid.

His fat jelly middle has become runny. His face looks like it's falling apart. His mouth has melted and spread across the ground. His eyes pop out dangerously.

'Bhaiya!' Lila comes running to us, out of breath. 'Kungfu Aunty just made the Black Dragon All Sweep move.' She pants, hands on knees, catching her breath.

'And?'

'I...I think we should leave. *Now*.'

I don't ask why. One look at the Trash Rajah's spreading goo and I know Lila's right. We gather the remaining trashball team and head to the exit.

None of the monsters stop us. They're too busy figuring out what is happening to their king.

The stadium rumbles as we dash down the mountain. The planks leading to the city creak under our feet. None of the monsters follow us.

We reach the mainland and join other humans who had escaped before us. Puke Peak groans and shakes.

'Oh, a park!' exclaims Granny Gee. She grins, and sits on a bench, looking at the lake. 'It'll be nice to go for a walk.'

'What's Black Dragon?' I ask Lila.

'You will see,' she says.

The whole island grumbles and shakes some more. Fleshy pieces of trash fly about in all directions like fireworks. Monstrous hollers and shrieks shoot out. A few fatflies and monsterquitoes fly up into the skies. The Black Dragon is here.

'Everyone! Move back!' shouts Dad. He grabs me and Lila and starts to run away from the lake.

'No!' Lila shakes off his hand and heads back to look at Puke Peak.

'Aunty!' she shouts, looking up in the skies. There's a lot of smoke there, a lot of pieces of floatsam, but no Kungfu Aunty.

There's an impossibly loud blast. Palace of Fume falls. The mainland quakes as the whole island shudders and sinks into the lake.

For a moment, the palace floats on the sludgy lake, before starting to sink into the lake.

'Aunty!' cries Lila.

'It's over, Lila,' says Dad, taking her into his arms.

'No!'

The island disintegrates. From the smoke and debris, something spirals out. A rocket. A bird. No, Kungfu Aunty. She twists and turns, dancing as she zaps the leftover monsters in the skies around her.

It's beautiful. Like thunder and rain.

# THE KUNGFU ARMY

Trash Rajah is gone. Pretty City's streets are cleaner. Our lake is blue, our trees have fresh green leaves. Our skies have become bluer. Some days we can even leave home without wearing oxyhelms.

For now.

All humans—kids and adults—have come together to make sure they keep the city clean. For I'm sure the monsters will come back if we don't clean our homes, our streets, our parks, our buildings, our city. So we prepare. All of us, the students of Pretty City School have joined the Kungfu Army.

After school, we have work. We make sure that no one throws rotten food in the streets.

We use public transport and cycle to school. All industries that were running to pollute now produce biobots and dustbins. We don't throw plastic, metal and glass into the lake. We scrub, we clean and we use air-filters to make sure viruses keep away from our lungs. We divide our waste into biodegradable and recyclable. We have strict laws for trash disposal.

And a lot of dustbins.

Granny Gee whacks anyone who grumbles about using dustbins. 'Dustbins keep the garbage monsters away,' she says.

Principal Ashraf has also taken to cleaning with a passion. The school has become sparkling clean. Anyone who as much as throws a wrapper on the floor is given detention.

Gardener Kaka adapted very well to greening our playground and has planted all kinds of beautiful flowers in the flowerbeds—marigolds, roses, daisies, jasmine, frangipani and my favourite, lavender.

After Trash Rajah's monsters vanished from the city, Mayor Junkfan came to Dad, begging for forgiveness. Dad being Dad, forgave the traitor. Since then, the mayor has helped Dad open up a museum for Mom's inventions and a factory to develop them. Mom's biobins and cleanbots are being sold all over the world.

Playing without oxyhelms, my football team (we discarded all terms related to trash) has become better. Meera thinks I'm still a hero, though I disagree. I'm still a fan of Wild Wuss. Vedika continues to be good at both math and being our forward. Recently, we won a match against Daffodils Private School!

After fighting with Trash Rajah and his monsters, Ishani, Ayaan and Virat have given up bullying. Instead, they all have become Lila's fan and now follow her around everywhere.

That brings me to my annoying little sister. In the year since Kungfu Aunty came into our lives, she has grown up. With nothing to rebel against, the eight-year-old now confidently gives instructions to people in their sixties and to the rest of the school. She does meetings with resident associations. She is also in the cleaning committee of our neighbourhood. They all listen to her. She's a hero. In another year, she might just become the mayor.

Since the city has become so clean and the humans are doing a good job, Kungfu Aunty has retired. She has gone to the rubble that used to be Palace of Fume. It still exists, in one corner of Pretty Lake (we changed that name too). Kungfu Aunty lives in the building, cleaning up remnants of Trash Rajah's palace. It's therapeutic to her, Lila tells me. I also heard that Kungfu Aunty has a few captives in the palace. One of them is a certain captain we used to know.

When Lila wants to play, she and I hang out in Mom's lab and create new inventions to tackle garbage. Or we use the controller, call Kungfu Aunty and watch martial art movies from my Mom's collection.

My pesky little sister. I guess she's not *that* bad.

# ★ ACTIVITY ★

## LILA'S LIST OF KUNGFU AUNTY'S GIFTS

Draw the garbage fighting tools that Lila's Mom created. Which one is your favourite?

Nano Scrub: Deep clean and tackle grime

Woozy Wand: Spritz into a monster's eye to put them to sleep.

Citronella Atomizer: Spray a monsterquito to make them fall.

Rapid Rot: Decompose biodegradable waste at supersonic speeds.

QuickGro Seeds: Seeds that make a tree in a jiffy.

Sonicbroom: Suck Particulators and Virulates out of the skies.